KU-506-724

MAKING YOUR GARDEN PAY

Also by Ian G. Walls
Tomato Growing Today

MAKING YOUR GARDEN PAY

Profit from Garden and Nursery

IAN G. WALLS

and

A. S. HORSBURGH

DAVID & CHARLES
NEWTON ABBOT   LONDON
NORTH POMFRET (VT)   VANCOUVER

0 7153 6365 4

© Ian G. Walls and A. S. Horsburgh 1974

All rights reserved. No part of this publication may be reproduced, stored in a retrieval system, or transmitted, in any form or by any means, electronic, mechanical, photocopying, recording or otherwise, without the prior permission of David & Charles (Holdings) Limited

Set in 11 on 13pt Baskerville and printed in Great Britain for David & Charles (Holdings) Limited South Devon House Newton Abbot Devon

Published in the United States of America by David & Charles Inc North Pomfret Vermont 05053 USA

Published in Canada by Douglas David & Charles Limited   3645 McKechnie Drive West Vancouver BC

Contents

Contents

Illustrations

PART I

Getting Started

An Introduction to Growing Crops for Profit

There must have been many gardeners, both young and old, with visions of the idyllic rapture and therapeutic benefits of grappling with the forces of nature in earning a living from the soil.

We have no wish to deter anyone with such enthusiasm, but in this book we do hope to set down in practical and realistic terms the facts and figures involved in many kinds of commercial horticulture. At the same time we will take into account the more intangible returns possible from a well-organised garden, in the form of fresh tasty fruit and vegetables, home-made wines, and a wealth of flowers for floral art, apart from the sheer aesthetic beauty of the garden as a whole. Success in anything can surely best be defined as the outcome of a satisfactory level of existence and way of life, doing something which one really enjoys. Perhaps this is why there are so many aspirants for the horticultural industry: it seems to offer so much as a way of life.

Translating the many imponderables which must exist in any horticultural venture into practical terms requires, in addition to horticultural skills, good business acumen, as it does in any other industry; and never perhaps in the whole history of horticultural production has this been more the case than it is today. No amount of theory can be a substitute for the more practical experience of actually running a business, and while this is a philosophy which can apply to any walk of life, it is particularly pertinent in the whole sphere of horticulture, where one has not only to produce the required item under varying conditions of weather, but at the end of the day market it successfully.

Here we take a critical look at the range of crops which can be grown, the modern methods of producing them, and at the end of the day the possible income or profit likely to result.

Ian G. Walls
A. S. Horsburgh

Glasgow 1973

Note
'Margins' for any given crops are readily obtained by offsetting all direct costs against probable yields and returns, and this was done at the time of going to press. Labour content is obtained by examination of the agreed cultural programme.

A glossary of terms and their definitions used in the text of this book is given on p 212.

CHAPTER 1

An Assessment of Resources— Climate, Land and Finance

No one should surely try to do anything without an assessment of his resources and of whether he has any real chance of achieving his aims and objectives. Buying a house, car, or anything, involves strictly factual calculations of how much money one has or is prepared to borrow over the years, and of whether one is capable of continuing to earn sufficient money to meet what are usually increasing liabilities.

Making a decision on whether to start a horticultural enterprise is, however, much more complex, as apart from the initial and necessary capital requirement (see p 18) there are factors of climate, soil and suitable equipment to be considered, and last but certainly by no means least the technical knowledge has to be found to be able to synchronise all the various factors.

CLIMATE

Precise locality and the prevailing climate exert a profound influence on the horticultural pattern of any area, and although this is an elementary matter, it is something all too frequently overlooked when people make their gardening plans. Horticulture is too often projected as a precise science, especially if crops are to be grown under glass, one that will proceed irrespective of the vagaries of the weather; this is certainly not the case. There are favourable and unfavourable areas for different crops, not only out of doors but under glass (see below).

The intensity of light is a vital matter for all green growing plants which depend on light for the photosynthetic process which takes place in their leaves. The actual strength or intensity of light controls the speed of photosynthesis to a very large extent, provided there are not other inhibiting factors—which will be discussed shortly.

Light, as we know, is derived from the sun, and solar energy consists of both light and heat. Areas which are sunny over the full year are of course generally warmer, unless they are extremely exposed. The intensity of light is of particular importance for the production of light-loving crops during the duller winter months.

Apart from the sheer complications and unpleasantness of working in the rain, there are the problems of soil cultivation to think about in an extremely wet area. Conversely, very dry areas can give rise to problems also for many crops, unless an irrigation system or at least watering facilities are to hand. There are of course the effects of rainfall on growth patterns, causing lush unproductive growth on fruit trees, encouraging disease in soft fruit crops, physically damaging flower crops, and many other issues. Many warm wet areas are of course ideal for the production of trees and shrubs.

Still another aspect of weather is the vital one of exposure, which affects all crops with equal severity; in many coastal or high-altitude areas the provision of effective shelter is essential before any horticultural enterprise can proceed. Even glasshouse units will be affected by exposure, which cannot only result in damage to structures, but can raise the heat loss, with considerable effect on fuel bills.

Exposure problems occur regionally and locally, but it would be difficult to overlook them in any problem area; the natural cover or vegetation of such regions will tell its own story. Some low-lying areas are well known for their coldness and in addition seem to catch the first and last frosts of the season with monotonous regularity. Such areas act as sumps for heavier colder air which develops due to the heat-exchange process which occurs when a cool, clear, cloudless night follows a warm day. This cold air fills up the frost pockets, causing crop damage, when adjacent areas may be unaffected, being above the 'cold-air-line'. These frost-pocket areas can make the growing of fruit bushes or trees, mid-season chrysanthemums, dahlias and other flowers hazardous.

A further climatic consideration is the slope of the land, which can determine whether or not early crops can be grown. In the northern hemisphere, south-facing land is much better angled for the absorption of sun heat than north-facing land, and while this may seem a trivial matter it can make a great difference in crop timing. It must not be thought, however, that only south-facing land is suitable for horticultural activities, as land in any aspect will have its uses, possibly for extending a crop's marketing period.

SOILS AND THEIR DRAINAGE

It is commonly known that soils are derived from the long-term weathering of the earth's crust and consist of different-sized mineral particles, with a quantity of organic matter derived from the decomposition of plant and animal remains over countless years and charged with countless numbers of micro-organisms. According to their derivation, age and whether developed in situ or transported by water or glacial movement, soils vary greatly in type, depth and proficiency in producing certain crops. Peaty soils are excellent for growing celery, whereas sandy soils produce superlative carrots. Clay soils (fine-particled) can, on the other hand, be not only extremely difficult to cultivate, but very inhospitable for many crops. The ability of certain soils to produce good crops will be fairly common knowledge in specific areas, and here is one case where soil analysis coupled with advice from a consultant or advisory officer would be valuable.

The drainage of land and whether it has a high or low water-table is also highly important and here again specialist advice should be sought.

WEEDS, PESTS AND DISEASES

With such a galaxy of modern chemicals and soil-cultivation equipment now available, one might be tempted to ignore the presence of weeds in land intended for intensive horticultural production. This would be folly, as while it is true that weed-controlling chemicals have reached an advanced stage of sophistication, it takes time and money to apply them and furthermore deal effectively with some of the more obnoxious weeds. Some expert assessment of the weed potential in any area of land is, we feel, an essential prerequisite for any intensive horticultural activity. So is an investigation into the pest and disease potential, potato eelworm determination being possible by an eelworm-cyst count, strawberry and potato eelworm being related partly to previous cropping history; the same is true to a certain extent with other pests and diseases such as club root, phytophthora of nursery stock, etc. A little patience in these matters can pay big dividends.

SERVICES AND LOCATION

The importance of having good water supplies and electricity conveniently to hand cannot be over-emphasised with any nursery project. All too often glasshouses are erected to be cropped 'cold', then in a year or so when more ambitious cropping is intended, the high cost of installing electricity to operate oil-fired boilers, for ventilation and for irrigation systems can come as a tremendous shock and make a big dip in capital reserves—although in most cases installation charges can be spread over a period. The same can also be said of water supplies and drainage outlets. Roadways, access and of course proximity to markets must be given careful consideration.

ADVICE

Agriculture and horticulture are industries which are particularly well served for advice, either through the official advisory services or through private consultants.

Much wrong advice can be given by well-meaning amateurs who, however successful they may be in winning prizes at flower shows, have had little opportunity for real insight into the true situation of running a horticultural enterprise for profit. Advisory officers are, in the main, a highly experienced group of people, backed by specialist services, who take great pride in seeing a successful unit being developed. They have their fingers firmly on the pulse of the horticultural industry of the area and know what opportunities exist. These are the people who can answer your questions.

FINANCIAL RESOURCES

There is a vital difference between a part-time and a full-time enterprise. In the former case land will usually be part of a heritable property, bought with money borrowed from a building society. Alternatively both the house and the land may be rented from a landlord. In both cases there is usually no surplus of capital available for business enterprise and it must therefore be procured from other sources. With a full-time enterprise it is usually possible to obtain capital more readily, especially on the value of land or on the strength of the established trading pattern over the years. In the case of a small part-time enterprise the capital required can usually be found from savings, especially where one also has a good

B

salary; in many cases money from family sources can be acquired or family property used for a loan guarantee. The following account of grants and capital sources is more applicable to someone already involved in a horticultural enterprise on either a part-time or a full-time basis, than for someone starting from the beginning.

Government Grants

Grant aid under the Horticultural Improvement Scheme was available in the UK until July 1973, provided eligible conditions could be met, to full-time horticultural businesses. From 1 January 1974 two new schemes were introduced. These are the Farm and Horticultural Development Scheme and the Horticultural Capital Grants Scheme. Details of these schemes are available from the Ministries of Agriculture in England, Wales and Northern Ireland, or from the Department of Agriculture and Fisheries for Scotland and advisory officers of the respective bodies. It is also possible that various other grants may be introduced from time to time according to changing conditions within the EEC.

Grant regulations usually specify that the business be viable, providing full-time employment for its owner or a person employed by the owner. Part-time nurseries are therefore not generally eligible for grant aid under the present regulations.

Estimating your Capital Requirements

Items such as glasshouses and heating systems involve high capital costs. They can be calculated easily once firm estimates have been received from the manufacturers concerned. An important point to watch if there is a grant available is that any delay in payment will increase the amount of capital required in the shorter term. Arrangements for a 'bridging loan' can be fairly easily obtained from one's bank to cover the period from when payments to suppliers are due and grants received. Additional working capital may be required to cover the cost of such items as fuel, wages, and materials, until the income starts to come in. Consideration must therefore be given to these shorter-term capital needs, particularly in certain types of businesses such as garden centres where large stocks of plants and materials have to be carried.

Calculating the Credit Needs of a Business
The best way of calculating the amount of credit needed by a business is by means of what is called a 'cash-flow' budget. This can be done by putting a date (approximate will do) against each item of expenditure and income over a period of say 2–3 years starting with the balance of cash available (if any). This makes it possible to calculate not only the total amount of credit needed but also the period for which it will be required.

The following example illustrates how a simple cash flow can be used as a guide to the future credit needs of a business. The flow of cash into and out of the business is given for a series of six monthly periods. It is assumed that the 'cash surplus' is not required to meet any part of living expenses etc. but would be available entirely to repay borrowed capital. Any liability for tax should be taken into account.

	Expenditure			Income			Cash srpls	Balance
								+=cash available
Period	Trdng Capital	Ttl expenses	(A)	Trdng Capital*	Trdng income	Ttl (B)	(−) Deficit (B)−(A)	−=credit required
Start	—	—	—	—	—	—	—	(+) £500
0–6 months	£1000	£100	£1100	—	—	—	(−)£1100	(−) 600
6–12 ,,	1000	400	1400	£700	—	£700	(−) 700	(−) 1300
12–18 ,,	—	600	600	200	£800	1000	(+) 400	(−) 900
18–24 ,,	—	400	400	—	200	200	(−) 200	(−) 1100
24–30 ,,	—	500	500	—	1000	1000	(+) 500	(−) 600
30–36 ,,	—	300	300	—	200	200	(−) 100	(−) 700
36–42 ,,	—	400	400	—	1100	1100	(+) 700	—

*Example only.

In this example the total fixed capital, paid in two equal instalments, amounts to £2,000 of which £900 is covered by grant aid. This leaves £1,100 to be found by the grower, either from his own resources or by borrowing. With £500 available in cash, a loan of £600 is needed to cover the balance of the fixed capital. Delay in payment of the grant together with other trading expenses incurred increases the amount of borrowing required up to a maximum of £1,300. The cash-flow budget, apart from providing an accurate assessment of the amount of borrowing required, is also a useful means of presenting this information to a prospective lender.

Credit Availability

Any discussion about the availability and cost of credit facilities must be viewed against the background of the economic conditions facing the country. Efforts to maintain the value of the pound sterling, or other currency linked with the problems of inflation, has resulted in high interest rates and require repaying the loan within a defined period. The cash-flow budget described earlier is a useful way of presenting this information as well as calculating the total credit needed. For the grower who can provide the necessary security and/or demonstrate his ability to make good use of any loans granted, there would seem to be adequate credit facilities available.

Private loans may be arranged on the same broad philosophy.

CHAPTER 2

Horticultural Training

Many countries have little tradition of horticulture and while this cannot be said of Britain, the United States or other developed countries, one must be truthful and say that the impact of commercial horticulture has in many ways been unfavourable and that the horticultural industry as a whole enjoys a poor image.

HORTICULTURAL EDUCATION AT SCHOOL LEVEL

This is clear when one compares the situation with that in, say, the Netherlands, where the horticultural industry has long been considered so important within the industrial framework of that country that horticultural education in schools has been widely accepted over generations. Yet until fairly recently in the UK, for example, there was no specialised horticultural education provided at school level, and general science and botany formed the only background for many in the middle age-group. It is unfortunate that the image remains of agriculture and horticulture being occupations for the less-intelligent person, despite the fact that the technological advances in agriculture and horticulture in the last decade have been so tremendous that it requires young people of high intelligence to cope with the sophisticated equipment now commonplace in production establishments.

Such thinking is, however, merely background to the practical problem of equipping oneself adequately to cope with some sphere of crop production with sufficient intensity to make it worthwhile.

PART-TIME EDUCATION

Part-time horticultural education is available in most centres, but in many cases much of this tends to be of a very general nature and confines itself more to the 'three Rs' of crop production—soils, manures and basic crop husbandry procedures. Commercially based classes dealing with crop production in detail are available in areas with intensive horticultural production. Day-release classes, including those under the aegis of Training Boards, are in operation for people employed in most industries, in the UK at any rate, and horticulture is no exception, but these are obviously not of so much interest to the person fully employed in another industry or profession. Short courses involving part-time education taken during holidays are one alternative, and while these tend to be infrequent, specialised in context and not generally systematic, they may well suit the person who has already specialised as an amateur grower in some aspect of production for many years.

FULL-TIME HORTICULTURAL EDUCATION

Full-time courses are available at many centres (see Appendix 4) and these range from certificate courses to those offering or leading to a degree or diploma. City & Guilds in various stages are now operative in horticulture right up to the Higher National Diploma level, but while these exams offer gradual progress up the educational ladder and give a sound general horticultural education, they do not necessarily synchronise with ambitions towards a commercial horticultural enterprise on one's own; they are more geared to giving higher qualifications to people wanting more lucrative employment within the horticultural industry. Business training is now becoming increasingly important and is usually included in full-time courses.

FULL- OR PART-TIME WORKING

Obviously one of the best ways of learning at a practical level about horticultural production is to take a job in an existing horticultural business, even on a part-time basis and there are now many more opportunities for working in nurseries in the EEC countries.

CORRESPONDENCE COURSES

Correspondence courses provide an excellent theoretical background to practical application and may well suit many. Progression from correspondence courses to an Open University course is possible, but here again one is equipping oneself more for an educational horticultural appointment, a matter rather outside the scope of this book.

Many gardeners with land at their disposal have started by growing a few strawberries or raspberries and then a few other crops, until they ended up with a large-scale full-time business. One could, for example, start off growing flowers such as dahlias or chrysanthemums for exhibition, then gradually develop into cut flowers for sale. Many heather or heath enthusiasts start off as amateurs before starting to propagate young stock for sale, the same being true of bedding plants and other lines. Countless thriving horticultural businesses began in this way and it can still be done today, provided one has the backing of a secure salaried post or other business to sustain oneself financially in the process.

CHAPTER 3

Enterprise Selection

Our purpose now is to examine the various forms of horticultural enterprises which could be embarked upon, and link them as far as possible to the type of person likely to become involved. Particular attention will be paid to the background of the person involved and his or her age group.

FEASIBILITY STUDIES

Making sure that one is setting out to produce items for which there is a demand, either locally or regionally, is something requiring very careful study. Is there reason for more production, and in what lines?

When one is considering the investment of a large amount of capital for horticultural production, a useful procedure is to carry out a 'feasibility study'. Such studies take various forms, some being fairly costly if done professionally.

PRODUCTION OF FRUIT, FLOWERS AND VEGETABLES FOR HOME USE ONLY

Most gardeners engage in this activity in one form or another, with varying degrees of intensity. There can be no set pattern of production, as personal preference, in association with what the garden will best grow, largely dictates the range of crops grown.

To put a value on the produce produced is not easy, although we have given some guidance (page 27). Obviously

too one cannot look too closely at the labour involvement, as
therapeutic or hobby principles have a large part to play,
especially with the person who works indoors or has almost
reached retirement age.

Quality and freshness cannot be ignored, especially now
that an increasing amount of crops are grown with much
reliance on chemicals, although gardeners should look closely
at their own production methods before being too critical of
'chemical' methods. The widespread use of deep-freezers, the
increasing interest in home wine-making, and for that matter
the popularity of floral art, all make home gardening attractive, although it is difficult to put all this in monetary terms.
Value of production from an average-sized fully utilised
suburban garden (eight houses to the acre) can be roughly
estimated as follows:

Outdoor Crops Only
Typical consumption figures for a family of four are given
below, together with an estimate of the areas required for each
crop. It is assumed the area available would be divided thus:

	Total area of garden	—	600sq yd
Less	House, driveways and Paths	—	200sq yd
	Front garden (cut flowers)	—	100sq yd
Area available for fruit and vegetables		—	300sq yd

Crop	Typical consumption per year*	Value (1 year) £	Yield per square yard	Area required sq yd
Potatoes	200lb	4.00	5lb	40
Cauliflower	25	2.50	2	13
Cabbage	72lb	2.80	3lb	24
Brussels sprouts	29lb	1.50	1½lb	20
Peas—fresh and for freezing	72lb	8.50	1¼lb	60

Crop	Typical consumption per year*	Value (1 year) £	Yield per square yard	Area required sq yd
Carrots	40lb	0.60	6lb	7
Onions and leeks	20lb	1.00	3lb	7
Turnip	16lb	0.20	2lb	8
Lettuce (summer)	40	2.50	5	8
Celery	25	1.75	3	8
Syboes	25bdl	1.00	5bdl	4
Strawberries, fresh, freezing and jam	30lb	4.00	11lb	30
Raspberries, fresh, freezing and jam	30lb	4.00	1lb	30
Apples—dessert and cooking	70lb	6.00	3lb	23
Plums	20lb	2.00	2lb	10
Flowers and misc produce		5.00		
		£47.35		292

*Based partly on National Food Survey figures.

Annual costs for fertiliser, sprays and a share of the cost of establishing the fruit trees and bushes would amount to less than £10, leaving a surplus of about £35. In fact the saving in the household budget could be higher if garden produce is substituted for expensive items such as tinned or frozen fruit and vegetables. This does assume, however, that a deep freeze is available so that produce such as peas and soft fruit can be used throughout the year. Substantial savings can also be made by using home-grown fruit for wine making.

Glasshouse and Outdoor Crops
A glasshouse measuring 6ft × 10ft and costing somewhere in the region of £50–£60 complete with a heating unit would be sufficient to provide most of the glasshouse produce required to feed a family of four. The glasshouse might also be used to raise plants for transplanting out of doors. This should make it possible to extend the season of some crops such as lettuce. A cold frame for hardening-off the plants would also be required.

The outdoor area could be used much as before, perhaps with a slightly earlier crop of lettuce transplanted in March or April. This could fill the gap in May and June and leave the glasshouse available for an early crop of tomatoes. About 20 lettuce worth about £1.50 would be required. These would fit into a rotation with the leek crop.

The value of the produce from the glasshouse is given in the table below:

Crop	Typical production per year	Value per year £	Total area used sq ft
Tomatoes (summer)	40lb	7.20	60 approx
Cucumber (summer)	5	0.60	1
Lettuce (winter)	40	3.00	20
		£10.80	

Value of outdoor produce (including early lettuce)	=	£48.85	
Total value of produce		=	£59.65
Less Cost of materials and fuel		=	£16.00
	Surplus		£43.65

HOME GARDENING WITH SALE OF SURPLUS

Many gardeners unwittingly indulge in this to a greater or lesser degree. Winning prizes at exhibitions, flower shows, etc, brings in some money with little actual profit, as the cash is usually ploughed back into the garden again—subsidising a hobby. Income tax, and still more important Value Added Tax, confuse the whole issue of selling surplus material other than food, and one would be better to get advice from an accountant before becoming too deeply involved. Income-tax authorities are, however, not usually concerned with the infinitesimal amount involved, particularly as it could be shown quite authentically in the majority of cases that anything received only goes in a small way towards paying for the cost of production. Monetary awards gained at flower shows are in effect an income directly related to garden production, and how many gardeners declare this? The intensive gardener is strongly advised to keep a careful record of all sales and where possible relate direct production costs to this, especially for items such as soft fruit, which can be quite considerable.

Where the scale of operations does not merit turning to a professional accountant for advice, one can do no better than contact the local tax authorities, who in our experience adopt an extremely realistic attitude. The situation of a person or persons on low income could be entirely different from that of a person with a high income.

PART-TIME PRODUCTION

There will always be criticism of the part-time operator in any business, and horticulture is no exception. Some of the main critics of the part-time operator are undoubtedly the large-scale producers who complain about what is called 'subsidised produce', as it is grown by someone who already has a main income from another job: this usually means that he is prepared to sell his produce cheaper and undercut the full-time producer. Deeper examination of the term 'part-time producer' will, however, show that a great many categories exist under this heading. Many professional people —lawyers, doctors, etc—also own farms or nurseries, many garden-centre operators are in fact glorified shopkeepers producing only a fraction of what they sell. Most Government-financed research stations and colleges produce crops and sell them. Conversely, many nurserymen have other associated business interests, selling agencies, tearooms, pubs, hotels, petrol stations and so on. The opening of large private establishments to the public, both for their beauty and for the purpose of selling their produce, is now commonplace, as indeed is the introduction of many other forms of activity. Even National Trust gardens sell various items. It is a free-for-all, but there are some rules, chiefly centring around buying and selling price-structures. There is in any case such specialisation creeping into some aspects of horticultural production that it is almost impossible for the small part-time producer to compete in uniformity of quality or price—or even if he can, the impact he makes is infinitesimal. Membership of the EEC throws further emphasis on this. One could of course argue that the quality of the small producer is higher, which is sometimes the case and can be turned to good advantage.

FULL-TIME PRODUCTION OF CROPS

Where the full-time growing of fruit, flowers or vegetables is undertaken, with sale of produce retail or wholesale, scale of production and area of land is important, along with capital for glasshouses and production equipment where this is necessary. More consideration is given to these matters in later chapters when the scale of operations necessary to bring in sufficient return for full-time working will be discussed. It must be appreciated, however, that considerable skill is necessary to grow crops well and that this will invariably demand a period of training.

JOBBING AND LANDSCAPE GARDENING

While not directly related to the growing of fruit, flowers or vegetables, jobbing gardening is in a way an extension of one's own garden, using such skill as one has acquired for the purpose of maintaining other people's gardens. Simple chores such as digging, lawn and hedge cutting, and general tidying-up are beyond the scope of many older people and some deeply involved business or professional people. In any district where there are high-class houses with large gardens there is tremendous scope for jobbing gardeners, and the basic rate varies according to district, being at the time of writing around 50p–70p per hour average.

As distinct from jobbing gardening, landscape gardening is something which is often—not always wisely—undertaken by amateurs. Simple layouts, making paths, lawns, rose beds, etc, can be undertaken by a reasonably competent amateur gardener, and some can be skilled at specialised cultivation with rock gardens, herbaceous borders and the like—but in the main, landscape construction on a large scale is the task of the well-equipped professional.

One can of course attend classes and train oneself for more ambitious landscape gardening with excellent results. One basic problem of landscape gardening on a professional scale is continuity of work and bringing in payment for work completed promptly enough, to avoid difficulty with capital resources.

FLORAL ARTISTRY

Many women in particular have become highly skilled at floral art and have, in consequence, moved into either full- or part-time floristry. Many also grow a good deal of the decorative material needed in their own gardens, not only to reduce costs but ensure a convenient supply of material. Lecturing is frequently undertaken, and this again demands material in large and continuous quantities. Training-classes for floral art are run in most areas, and this is usually the best way to start on a part-time basis, although for those anxious to take up full-time floristry, 'apprenticeships' can often be arranged.

Success in floristry depends much on sheer ability, and competition can be intense.

GARDEN CENTRES

'Garden Centres' have become very much a part of the British way of life in the last ten years or so, having developed in the USA a great many years ago. To become an 'Approved Garden Centre', under the specifications laid down by the British Horticultural Trades Association, involves having adequate car parking, toilets, a complete range of well-presented produce ranging from shrubs to house plants, and a comprehensive selection of tools, equipment and garden sundries.

Many so-called 'Garden Centres' are simply huts selling fruit, flowers and vegetables and little else, on a seasonal basis, whereas the intensive Garden Centre is open for the whole year with its extensive range and continuity of produce. Obviously a massive capital injection is needed to build and equip a sophisticated Garden Centre, which after all is really a 'horticultural supermarket'. It should also be borne in mind that retail selling involves the employment of full-time staff, yet a basic problem with all Garden Centres is their seasonal nature. Diversification is therefore required, into a wide range of products and activities sometimes well beyond the sphere of gardening.

Roadside selling is common in many areas, particularly with strawberries, cherries and flowers, and obviously there is scope for a limited amount of this in most districts, although one should pay attention to local by-laws and the need to make income-tax returns.

A trend in recent years, in the USA particularly, has been a move away from Garden Centres into seasonal selling with existing sales staff in car parks of super and hypermarkets.

CARAVAN PARKS AND CAMPING SITES

The owners of land in areas of high rural beauty could do worse than consider development into a caravan park or camping site, the former being a year-round project in many cases, and the latter seasonal. Study of the regulations involved is needed before starting any developments, as a fairly high investment will be demanded to provide the appropriate services.

CHAPTER 4

Budgeting

It is necessary to have a certain amount of land and equipment to produce crops to various levels (see part II). At the elementary stages the equipment can simply take the form of hand tools, barrows, trolleys and cultivators, moving to tractors, large sprayers and other items at a later stage. Where glasshouse cropping is concerned, serious thought must be given not only to their actual area but to the form or type of glasshouse and the equipping of it, where the scale merits, with automatic heating, feeding, watering and ventilating appliances. There are also such items as plastic greenhouses, tunnels and frames to consider (see page 202). All these must be included in your budget.

Land or Glasshouse Requirements
It is a fairly straightforward matter to calculate the area of land or glasshouse necessary to sustain production at different levels, by perusal of gross returns (page 192), with the proviso that there can be considerable increase in income when entirely retail selling is intended. If one takes the example of growing strawberries in a reasonably good area, free from inherent pests and diseases (see page 132), one can be sure that 1 acre of strawberries will yield on average 2–2½ tons, or much more in favourable areas. By offsetting the production costs one is left with the 'gross margin' figure, which although not profit shows surplus of income over the direct expenditure concerned with that particular crop. Making suitable adjustment where necessary for advantageous selling, it is possible

33

a

to assess in fairly accurate form what the total return is for any given area, assuming normal cropping, which in turn quite clearly shows the scale of operations necessary.

This is a task which must be done quite objectively, avoiding over-enthusiasm of the sort one sometimes indulges in when convincing oneself of the need to buy an expensive new car or other luxury item! It is much better to err well on the cautious side. There is also a considerable danger of crop planning 'in isolation'. If, for example, one decides to grow a quarter of an acre of strawberries, a crop which, it is thought, can be sold without any difficulty and possibly at good prices, then one must think in terms of mechanical equipment for cultivation, in addition to sprayers for weed control and all the usual hand tools. To take matters further, the quarter-acre of strawberries will yield a considerable bulk of fruit, and whether this has to be distributed to local shops or taken to the wholesale market it demands transport, probably a trailer, van or shooting-brake. Obviously it would *not* be an economically viable proposition to buy transport specially for small quantities of strawberries—which shows the danger of isolated crop-planning. Consideration must therefore be given simultaneously to other aspects of the enterprise and their needs for transport. Part-time operation alters the issue, as transport may well be required for one's main occupation.

To quote a further example, it may be decided to grow tomatoes, and one must refer to the returns per 1,000sq ft offset against production costs, 'gross margins'. Glasshouses cost money, and another important issue about capital investment is that whether one is considering the purchase of an existing glasshouse nursery, or of erecting a new glasshouse, capital is being tied up and this must yield a return commensurate with investment. Likewise also there will be capital expense involved in heating and watering equipment, and again all the ancillary items such as transport to take into account.

Labour Requirements

No mention has yet been made of labour requirements on a pro-rata basis and this obviously cannot be lightly dismissed as it determines precisely what one person *can* undertake in the time he is likely to have available (see page 38). A hidden danger here is to take the total available labour input without allocating it appropriately in terms of what will actually be needed at what time. In other words, there can be a concentration of labour needed at some stages of the crop's production, and this is not available from the labour force, then casual labour must be called in, and this can happen on any scale of operations.

The level of technical proficiency in producing crops in the first instance is also of vital importance and cannot be overlooked: all the crop returns showing in the tables throughout this book assume a high level of proficiency. Mr X may wish to grow chrysanthemums under glass without realising that he is ill-equipped technically to do so and that the capital investment in terms of supplying planting stock and fuel to grow the crop is well beyond what personal budgetry he may have optimistically undertaken. (The fact that even the most efficient and well-equipped horticultural producer can come to grief owing to extreme variation of prices received for produce shows up once again one of the major weaknesses of the industry as a whole.)

The number of permutations in deciding upon any enterprise are endless and there is much to be said for a strictly *impartial* budget prepared by someone who understands the whole background of the situation.

BUDGETING PROCEDURE

In a full-time horticultural business the return must be sufficient to provide the standard of living to which the grower and his family aspire. In a part-time business it may be the minimum return which would justify the time and effort put into it compared with some alternative occupation, the criterion in this case being the return per hour worked. The hobby gardener, on the other hand, may accept a low return per hour simply for the reason that he gets so much enjoyment from working in his garden. Any additional income he gets in this way may be used to buy some coveted plant or piece of equipment. Whatever the personal objectives—and it is essential that these should be clear right from the start—the best way to make sure that these have a reasonable chance of being achieved is to prepare a budget.

A budget is simply a plan expressed in financial and quantitative terms, and can be conveniently divided into two distinct parts:

(1) The market plan—what can be sold, in what quantity, at what price?

(2) The production plan—what can be produced, in what quantity and at what cost?

The Sales Forecast
The start of the budgeting procedure, therefore, is the preparation of a reasonably accurate sales forecast. This may be obtained in a number of ways including the following:

(a) Analysing past sales by market outlets.

(b) Surveying market outlets in order to form a picture of likely future demand.

(c) Obtaining an estimate of total consumption in a given area and calculating expected share of the market.

In a nursery or garden producing relatively stable items of diet which are sold through well-established market outlets, it is often possible to forecast sales reasonably accurately. For example a tomato grower can usually expect to sell all the tomatoes he can produce provided the quality is right. Prices too are reasonably predictable. The problem becomes more difficult in the case of nurseries dealing in luxury items which are subject to sudden and often violent changes in consumer demand. Producers of flowers, pot plants and other ornamental crops, also garden centres selling shrubs and garden requisites, are examples of businesses which are likely to find difficulty in preparing an accurate sales forecast on which to base production and purchasing plans. Production beyond the needs of the market can often result in a substantial loss, with the margin for error becoming smaller all the time.

While growers selling the more stable crops can base their future cropping plans almost entirely on past experience, others dealing in the more luxury items may need to keep a closer watch on consumer demand. In this case a market survey of some sort may be a better way of preparing the sales forecast. Yet another approach would be to estimate a nursery's share of the forecasted total sales in a particular area. This might be a useful method for a garden centre or retail nursery to assess the potential market for its products.

The Production Budget
Once it has been established what can be sold it is necessary to deal with the problem of what can be produced. The first essential is an assessment of the resources available—ie the amount of land, glasshouses and frames, labour and machinery, capital and credit. It is at this point that individual crop budgets can be prepared, based on the information in part II. These are offered, however, only as a general guide as to what should be achieved with modern equipment under reasonably good conditions and management. In the long run what is important is to discover the standards of performance which can be achieved under the conditions existing on the individual garden or nursery.

Example of Budget for a Part-time Nursery
In order to illustrate how to draw up a budget, an example

has been taken using a mythical nursery. The business is a part-time one and the owner and his wife are prepared to spend 20 and 15 hours a week on it, respectively, provided the income is not less than £25 per week—or about 70p per hour. The resources available are as follows:

Land	— 1½ acres good arable, medium loam.	
Glasshouses	— 1,000sq ft traditional wooden houses; oil-fired heating	
Labour	— Grower—20 hours per week Wife—15 hours per week	
Capital	— Cash balance	£200
	Additional overdraft facilities	£300
	Total	£500
Markets	— Good local wholesale outlets for vegetables and flowers. The nursery is not well situated for retail selling.	
Skills	— The grower has had only a few years experience of general market gardening. He has had no formal horticultural or business training.	

Reference to the summary tables (page 192) makes it possible to place alternative crops in order of highest margin per acre, per 1,000sq ft of glass, and per hour worked. It will be noticed that some crops which give a high margin per acre have a relatively high labour content and a low margin per hour worked. The best way is to start with crops which give the highest margin per square foot of glass and per acre. Once it is clear that the labour requirement is more than that available over a period of one or two months, it will be necessary to substitute with crops further down the list

which use less labour. An example illustrating the procedure
is given below:

List of crops in order of margin

	Margin	
	Per Acre	Per Hour
Chrysanthemums	1,559	0.79
Stocks	1,151	1.54
Radish	830	2.40
Lettuce—early	693	1.23
Onions	408	2.08

A glance at the monthly labour requirements shows that an
acre of outdoor chrysanthemums would use double the total
amount of labour available (150 hours) for three months of
the year. Even half an acre would use up most of the time
available and would only give a margin of £700–£800.
Stocks are a much better proposition, since apart from July
when the labour requirement climbs to over 300 hours, it
would be well within the capacity of the grower and his
wife. Once a tentative cropping programme has been worked
out, the next stage is to go round the various market outlets
to get the sales forecast. This might give the following result.

	Sales Forecast
Chrysanthemums	2,500 bunches
Stocks	2,500 bunches
Radish	No demand
Lettuce—early	2,000 dozen
Onions	20 tons
Tomatoes	500 boxes
Tulips—Christmas	1,500 bunches

From this information the cropping plan can be worked out
as follows:

Cropping Programme

Under glass	Area	Limiting Factors
Tomatoes	1,000sq ft	area of glass
Tulips—Christmas	300sq ft	market

Outdoor		
Chrysanthemums	$\frac{1}{4}$ acre	labour & market
Stocks	$\frac{1}{3}$ acre	market
Early lettuce	$\frac{2}{3}$ acre	market
Onions	$\frac{1}{4}$ acre	area of land

Labour requirements

Crop	Total	J	F	M	A	M	J	J	A	S	O	N	D
Tomatoes	131	4	8	15	17	10	24	18	16	10	2	5	2
Tulips	72	—	—	—	—	—	—	—	—	—	19	5	48
Chrysanthemums	496	38	28	18	13	75	43	30	25	88	88	50	—
Stocks	253	—	1	1	52	41	20	57	50	27	2	2	—
Early lettuce	370	67	60	42	42	60	65	—	—	—	—	14	20
Onions	49	—	—	1	—	1	—	3	2	2	—	—	40
Total	1371	109	97	77	124	187	152	108	93	127	111	76	110

Labour available = 150 hours per month

This table shows that the cropping programme is well within the capacity of the grower and his wife, with the exception of May and June when a little extra help may be needed.

At this stage detailed budgets can be drawn up for each crop in turn. Set down your target yield for the area where each will be grown, and the revenue (less commission) each is likely to bring in. List the crop expenses, item by item, and deduct the total from the revenue to reach your margin. Then with the addition of estimates for labour and other nursery expenses, a profit for the year ahead can be estimated. In addition the expected margin from the glass and outdoor land can be separately assessed.

Master Budget for Year Ahead

	Total	Glasshouse	Outdoor
REVENUE	£2163	£429	£1734

Less crop expenses

Seed, bulbs, cuttings	168	102	66
Fertilisers, peat, compost	54	15	39
Pots, boxes	3	3	
Soil sterilisation	10	10	
Fuel oil	113	113	
Twine, sprays, water, canes	27	4	23
Packaging	191	16	175
Carriage	115	12	103
	681	275	406
MARGIN	1482	154	1328

Less Nursery overheads

Casual labour, 40 hours @ 50p	20
Repairs & upkeep	100
Car expenses—$\frac{1}{6}$th	50
Sundry expenses	50
	220
TRADING PROFIT	£1262

RECORDS AND ACCOUNTS

If the method of budgeting outlined in the previous section is carried out and, even more important, properly used to establish high yet attainable standards of performance, there should be no need for a very elaborate system of records and accounts. Ideally a cash book should be kept for recording payments and receipts. If it has columns for analysing returns from each crop and payments for different items, this will give a check on the overall budget figures. The cash book will also ensure that adequate records are kept for tax purposes.

Additional records may be kept in order to check on the standards of performance which have been built into the budget. This is done by identifying the items which are likely to have a significant effect on the profit margin from the crop. By identifying these key figures the records can be designed to give information quickly and easily to compare with the budget. Obviously the sooner the grower is aware of differences between the actual and budgeted performance, the sooner he will be able to define the reasons and decide what corrective action he should take—next year if it is too late to do anything about the current year's crop.

Records which may be worth keeping on a regular basis are:

1. Crop yields
2. Fuel consumption (glasshouse crops)
3. Diary of important dates of sowing, planting and harvesting crops
4. Rates of working on the bigger jobs

CHAPTER 5

Equipping for Production

HAND TOOLS

Most gardeners with commercial ambitions will be familiar with hand tools! It is as well, however, to bear in mind that even these have been developed, particularly hoes and sprayers.

MECHANICAL EQUIPMENT

For soil cultivation on any scale some means of mechanical cultivation is essential.

Rotary Cultivators

Rotary cultivators in various sizes have become an accepted part of soil husbandry, and while older gardeners may abhor their intermixing as opposed to inversion principle and gloomily predict damage to soil structure, practical experience with cultivators over many years has proved otherwise. It is important to ensure an adequate supply of organic matter in the soil and to avoid using rotary cultivators when the soil is too wet. The depth achieved with a rotary cultivator is directly related to size and power, with cost also relative. The smaller lightweight rotary cultivator costing £70–£100 is capable of dealing with around half an acre and will achieve any reasonable depth. For larger areas, from one to two acres or more, heavy cultivators costing between £300–£400 give a more suitable handling performance and depth. Both a small and a large cultivator are essential for intensive cultivation on a fairly large scale, the former for inter-row work.

Several of the small cultivators are adaptable for ploughing, a current practice which does in part emulate digging as it inverts the soil, but the depth achieved depends on the power of the unit and the type of soil. Tractors, on the other hand, make an excellent job of ploughing and with a rotavator attachment rotavate the soil also; but they can be very expensive, a second-hand tractor costing as much as £400–£600.

One must be realistic about soil-cultivation equipment—investment in it should be commensurate with the scale of operations. While it is convenient to have one's own means of soil cultivation on tap, the actual amount of time a machine is used may be very limited, particularly with a small enterprise, and hiring a cultivator or tractor when required may be a much better proposition. Co-operative purchase of good machinery, while having its drawbacks, has many advantages.

What has been said about cultivators and tractors applies also to ancillary soil-cultivating equipment such as harrows and other items; highly specialised equipment should not be bought unless it can be economically justified. The tremendous savings provided by careful and selected purchase of secondhand equipment should not be overlooked.

Other Mechanical Equipment
Soil shredders, rotary drum or electric sterilisers and blockmakers are typical items likely to be found in a small general nursery, but once again their purchase depends on how much they will be used. Only where an enterprise involves the use of vast amounts of soil-based growing media will a soil shredder or steriliser be economically viable, and even then the use of soil-less mediums needing no sterilisation should be carefully considered. An automatic mechanical blockmaker using wet peat can only be justified where sufficient acreage of a crop such as lettuce is being grown, either under

glass or out-of-doors. The basis for decision on this matter is to look at the gross margin for each crop, with particular attention to the labour costs.

Lorries and Vans
The need for specialised transport for a horticultural enterprise depends almost entirely on operational scale. Far too often, in our experience, expensive lorries or vans are purchased when it would be better to hire transport as required or to use a trailer behind the car.

INSURANCE

Various aspects of insurance should always be investigated, not only in relation to equipment but to glasshouses and other items such as crop risks (although premiums can be high in this respect).

GRANTS

At the time of writing, various grants are available for equipment, glasshouses, installation of water, installation of roads, and on a wide range of items. (See Appendices for list of equipment and capital costs involved.)

CHAPTER 6

Greenhouses

The climatic considerations relating to light intensity, wind and warmth, have been referred to, and yet finding the ideal site where all the conditions are fully satisfied to maximise crop production would be difficult. Broadly speaking, any glasshouse on any site is capable of producing crops, but there are different types, having varying proficiency in producing different crops, with important economic overtones. One of the main considerations in any glasshouse is the ratio of glass to opaque material, which in more down-to-earth terms relates to the size of glass pane and the size of the structural members supporting it.

Older-type glasshouses erected on stout base walls, of which there are still many in existence, epitomise the heavy structured light-*excluding* glasshouse. In direct contrast, the modern alloy glasshouse with its large pane size, glass to ground level, and slender glazing bars or astragals admits maximum light. Yet the economic anomaly which arises is that glass must, by virtue of its basic function, be capable of transmitting sun heat, but this passage of heat is a two-way business and there is rapid heat loss through the glass when the sun ceases to shine and similarly rapid heat loss when artificial heat is used to raise the glasshouse temperature. With less total area of glass, provided that the glazing is tight and there are no exceptional air leaks, the older-type structure, although admitting less light, will in many cases conserve its heat much better than the modern glasshouse.

On balance, however, light is such an important consideration for most crops, except perhaps at some earlier stages of propagation, that there is much to be said for the all-glass structure, particularly when light-loving crops are to be grown in winter or early in the year.

ORIENTATION

Apart from the actual ratio of glass to glazing members, the orientation of a glasshouse is so important that this could well dictate its cultural role. Light is directional and in the northern hemisphere it is from a southerly aspect (the converse, of course, being true of the southern hemisphere). Glass is a reflective material and the maximum light and solar heat penetrates it when the angle of incidence is as near 90° as possible. In the winter months the sun's angle to the earth is so low in most temperate climates that it can be seen that there are obvious difficulties in achieving anything like the optimum transmission of light through the glass. For this reason there is considerable virtue in an east/west orientated glasshouse, which means that the long axis of the conventionally shaped glasshouse runs east/west, so presenting the vertical or slightly sloping south side to the low-angled sun. If the same glasshouse is turned north/south then only the south-facing gable-end is well placed for reception of light and sun heat, which has severe repercussions during the duller winter months. This is true of single and double span glasshouses, less so with multispan blocks of glasshouses, although here too recent experimental work has stressed the value of east/west siting.

Obviously glasshouse type and siting are critical factors which must be given very careful consideration whether it is an existing or a new nursery which is being developed. It is our experience that sometimes in the initial enthusiasm of a venture, such basic considerations are overlooked, with their financial implications, particularly when a nursery is

attractively priced, has a good dwelling house, or other
desirable features.

VENTILATION

When new glasshouses are being built, a much more
enlightened attitude to ventilation is now apparent to avoid
spoilage of crops with excess heat, high humidity or irregular
temperatures, it being usual to provide a ventilator ratio of at
least one-sixth, preferably one-fifth, of the floor area, to cool
the glasshouse effectively. Ventilators should preferably be
operated automatically on thermostat. Fans can of course be
installed in either new or old glasshouses, and are most effective in cooling glasshouses under all conditions and giving
excellent automatic control of the glasshouse environment.

HEATING

Heating systems must be adequate for the crop range intended
to be grown and in view of the variability of cropping patterns which may be essential to compete with European
countries within the Common Market, heating systems should
be of adequate capacity and designed for a large range of
crops, and must operate at high efficiency.

Few gardeners will have failed to note that large-bore
(4in or thereabouts) pipe systems are seldom, if ever, installed
in new glasshouse units. Many older glasshouses of course
still have the 4in pipe systems of cast iron or steel, a legacy
of the days when it was necessary to design a glasshouse
system on the gravity circulation principle, involving large-
diameter pipes containing the greater volume of water necessary to allow the warmer and lighter water to circulate by
rising to the highest point in the system, to return to the
lowest on cooling. The boilers or heat-producing units in
earlier days were invariably coal-fired and fuel was cheap, and

Page 49 (above) Simple gadgets can save time for the busy gardener. Here is a plastic nozzle for water distribution with a multiferous range of uses; (below) a small well-equipped modern greenhouse is an asset to any garden, commercial or otherwise. If heated it can be used for miscellaneous propagation of pot plants. Without heating or with benching removed the border can be used for growing crops such as lettuce, tomatoes or cucumbers.

Page 50
(*left*) A well displayed rang
of pot plants always attract
attention and invites sales.
Here Ivies, Peperomia,
Cyclamen, Stags Horn Fern
and Cyprus compete with
each other for attention;
(*below*) bulb growing can
embarked upon and in
various forms, from the
production of the bulbs
themselves to the production
of cut blooms for floral art
or sale.

in general the sluggish large water-volume systems were ideally suited to the slow output of heat from the coal. Once heated these large water-volume systems remained warm for a long period, which of course has virtues, especially when power cuts occur. Warm pipes during the day also help to circulate air.

But the large cumbersome nature of 4in pipes, the room they take, plus the difficulty of achieving even distribution of heat across the glasshouse area, and last but not least the time and cost taken to heat the volume of water contained in them, are all factors which have led to their abandonment. The high cost of large-diameter pipes, if indeed such pipes are still available, and their costly installation, must also be taken into account. The slowness of achieving uniform warmth in large-diameter pipes is technically termed '*high thermal inertia*'. Pipes of $1\frac{1}{4}$–2in diameter do not take up much room, can be 'spread' to give uniform warmth, and contain only about one-fifth of the volume of water of a 4in pipe system of similar BTU capacity. The thermal output of smaller-diameter pipes in the $1\frac{1}{4}$–2in range is about half that of 4in pipes. The one problem of small-diameter systems is the frictional resistance developed, necessitating a circulating pump, which has the advantage of pushing the heated water around the system quickly and also allowing the pipes to be run up and down as necessary without adhering to the steady rise and fall necessary with a gravity circulation system. Warm-air heating systems are much cheaper to install than pipe systems and operate at high efficiency. They can vary from convectors or fan heaters to large oil-fired or steam-heated warm-air units.

The subject of glasshouses, their ventilation and heating is one demanding some experience and one should not hesitate to ask for help from a consultant. Glasshouse firms, of which there are an increasing number, while of course obviously biased in their outlook towards glasshouses of their own manu-

D

facture, will nevertheless plan glasshouse projects in detail on paper and in addition sur~ey the intended site. All experienced *commercial* glasshouse firms are fully up to date on the matter of ventilation and may also have contacts for heating-system installations, offering in fact a 'package deal'; there is much to be said for this as it avoids dealing with a number of contractors.

Older glasshouses in a nursery which one is intending to purchase should be surveyed by a horticultural consultant or valuator who, in addition to checking stability, will report in detail on the efficiency of ventilation or heating facilities.

AMATEUR-SIZED GREENHOUSES

The distinction must be drawn between those firms manufacturing amateur-sized greenhouses and those specialising in commercial glasshouses. There are also some firms which manufacture specialist glasshouse units for Parks Departments at a price which bears no relation at all to the commercial glasshouse as an investment for crop production.

Most 'amateur' firms have no real background of large-scale glasshouse building, nor is it our experience that they are, generally speaking, suitably versed technically in ventilation and heating methods. The scale of operations is also a vital factor to take into account, there being a basic size of greenhouse which is scarcely economically viable, as will be seen by perusal of crop returns.

MAINTENANCE

Freedom from maintenance is a very important consideration with all glasshouses, as nothing can be more time-consuming and costly than the painting of glasshouses, inside and out! All modern wooden glasshouses are now built of wood which has been preservative-treated under pressure. Alternatively, aluminium alloy or galvanised steel is used. Glazing systems are either 'dry' or embody plastic sealing strips and clip and bar-cap methods, all features which reduce maintenance to the absolute minimum.

ACCESS

Access to and from glasshouses is also important, especially in strictly commercial terms where mechanised barrows or tractors may be used. Most modern commercial-sized glasshouses should have sliding doors wide enough to allow the entry of a tractor and trailer.

ERECTION

Any new greenhouse purchased should be simple to erect, this being possible by the sectional factory construction as opposed to building on location. Ready adaptation to automatic equipment, including ventilation control, has been referred to.

FEEDING AND WATERING SYSTEMS

Of tremendous importance in these days when every effort must be made to restrict labour costs is the use of watering and feeding systems of an automatic or semi-automatic nature. These can take the form of low or high level spray-lines or drip systems, according to cropping needs.

Care should be taken when installing dilutors that local water board regulations are adhered to in respect of feed-back contamination risk to the mains supplies, which may, in many instances for pressurised systems, demand separate reservoirs.

BENCH WARMING AND MIST PROPAGATION

Bench warming systems linked with mist propagation are

well worthy of consideration where intensive propagation is involved, as they are both efficient and economical.

THE CASE FOR MOBILE GREENHOUSES

Mobile greenhouses are not a new conception, having been developed as long ago as the early part of the century, and they have obvious economic advantages. They allow 'crop rotation' under glass, avoiding soil-sickness problems. While not so popular in recent years due to the efficiency and relatively low cost of chemical soil-sterilisation and alternative cultural methods for certain crops (see page 123), they nevertheless have an extremely useful role to play for the smaller unit where labour may be scarce and all aspects of time-saving highly important.

Basically a mobile greenhouse allows a crop such as lettuce to be grown in plot 1, after this, the greenhouse being pushed on to plot 2 when a crop of tomatoes is planted. In the meantime a crop of chrysanthemums is planted out in plot 3 in May, or plot 1 if this is cleared, and the greenhouse is pushed over them (the earlies left for crop clearance). Finally, there may still be time to cover a late crop of lettuce planted in the vacant plot. In subsequent years the crops are rotated so that a different area is allocated to each crop to avoid the build-up of specific troubles. Calculations made on the basis of total crop returns from a mobile greenhouse with commensurately low production cost form an impressive economic picture.

The number of permutations are endless, a very popular crop in Holland being early strawberries which are grown to a very large extent in mobiles, simply because the young newly rooted plants can be established out of doors in summer and have a period of vernalisation (low temperature) out of doors, before being covered in January or February. Various arrangements can be made for heating a mobile greenhouse, one of the most convenient being to use a warm-air unit which can fairly readily be moved.

PLASTIC STRUCTURES

Of very particular interest now are the various types of plastic greenhouses, structures of polythene or PVC which have been extremely popular both in much of Europe and in the USA for many years. In Britain they suffered a severe setback when first introduced with any seriousness about twenty years ago, largely because of the very rapid breakdown of the plastic by the ultra-violet content of light. Considerable research has now produced much more stable forms of plastic, including both the thin and thicker rigid grades. The thicker, rigid grades, although allowing the construction of curved-roof greenhouses with enhanced light transmission, are costly. Both 125mu and 150mu gauge polythene used on a relatively short-term basis is very inexpensive and much the same can be said about PVC. Earlier problems of securing the plastic and avoiding local stress-points have now been efficiently overcome, the most generally accepted type of structure today being the 'tunnel' in various widths, where the plastic is stretched over a series of semi-circular galvanised metal or rigid wooden hoops. The plastic can either be lapped into a trench on the ground or strained with various types of tensioners, which appears to avoid excess flapping and subsequent damage.

Plastic greenhouses can be self-built or purchased in kit form and, apart from the tunnels, are available in a wide variety of shapes and forms, including multi-span units.

A basic problem with all plastic greenhouses is ventilation, due to the condensation and precipitation of moisture on the inside of the plastic film, giving rise to moisture droplets and high humidity, although this can be completely overcome by effective fan ventilation, and to a lesser degree by 'double

skinning'. 'Bubble' greenhouses are a different type of structure and rely on pressurised air to keep them erected, ventilation being effected by an ancillary fan and a counterbalanced
outlet.

The low cost of the less-sophisticated plastic structures
makes them particularly attractive as a low-investment growing unit for a wide variety of purposes, including crops such
as tomatoes, with the provision of crop-supporting methods.
It is wise however to compare their cost over a few years with
a cheaper Dutch light form of traditional greenhouse.

There is also the crop risk involved, as plastic structures
are not as stable as a traditional greenhouse, especially in
exposed areas. Excess winds are, however, the exception
rather than the rule, except in exposed areas where even
traditional greenhouses may require to be specially
reinforced.

The use of plastic tunnels has developed considerably in
recent years. Relatively low cost is involved, with very considerable opportunity for profit by earlier production. The
price difference for a crop such as strawberries produced 10–
14 days earlier can be immense, the same being true of
lettuce produced both earlier and later into the autumn, and
the same could be said for a wide range of crops. Growers in
many countries have found tremendous advantage in plastic
tunnels and there are increasing areas of them to be seen in
many regions.

On a large scale the hoops are inserted manually and the
plastic laid from a tractor-mounted appliance, the plastic
being secured over the hoops by polypropylene twine. On a
small scale plastic tunnels can be self-made and hand-laid
without great expenditure of capital or labour.

One vital aspect of plastic-tunnel culture is overcoming
moisture supply to the crop and also allowing pollination in
the case of strawberries.

Glass cloches in various forms and shapes, including

elevated forms, have their place as a more permanent crop-forwarding device, and although the glass cloche tends to be vulnerable to wind damage, the elevated cloche or frame is a permanent unit capable of a wide diversity of crop production.

COLD FRAMES

There is conflict of design between the elevated cloche and the cold frame, the 'true blue' cold frame having originally been a 6ft × 4ft heavy wooden construction set on a low brick wall. Usually the frames were linked to a greenhouse on its southerly aspect (although there was a place for shaded frames also), this readily allowing heating pipes to be run from the greenhouse.

Many such cold-frame units still exist and are used to good effect, but anyone who has worked with these old-fashioned frames will know how cumbersome they are. The arrival of the 'Dutch light', measuring approximately 5ft × 2½ft overall, in the 1930s set a new pattern for frame culture. These single-pane glass units became very popular, being light to handle, and there must have been millions of them made to the original basic design which has never really been bettered. The first area in Britain to utilise Dutch lights in any quantity was the East Riding of Yorkshire where the Dutch immigrant growers originally settled, and here they were used on a wooden base in either single or double span forms for lettuce, cucumbers and other crops. The commercial success of such low-investment cropping, initially with Dutch lights and thereafter in Dutch-light structures, formed the cornerstone for many of the large and successful holdings which exist in the East Riding of Yorkshire and other areas today. There is a lesson to be learned from this, as success does not automatically follow from putting up the most expensive and sophisticated greenhouse.

MONTHLY GREENHOUSE UTILISATION CHART

CC = completely cool   FP = frost protection   H = very well heated

	J	F	Mh	A	M	J	Jy	A	S	O	N	D
Seed sowing, cuttings, bedding plants, etc. (H) (FP) (CC)												
Overwintering pot plants, dahlia tubers, etc (H & FP) (Not tender plants in FP)												
Tomatoes & cucumbers (H) ,, (FP) ,, (CC)												
Lettuce (all levels of heat) (later maturing without any)												
Utilisation of greenhouse generally (H)												
ditto (FP)												
Hardy crops												
Tender crops												
In winter (CC)												
Only for crops which are capable of existing out of doors in mild winters												

Lettuce are frequently grown on a year-round basis under glass for quality; there is in fact no limit to the range of crops which can be grown in heated greenhouses, much depending on the level of heat.

CHAPTER 7

Modern Technology in Perspective

Technical advances in most industries have, in the last twenty years or so, been dramatic, and the same is true of horticulture in many vital aspects, especially as far as chemicals are concerned. Organic principles of husbandry have however much to their credit, and indeed the gardener willing to study and follow the basic principles of organic husbandry where the biological cycle is allowed to function, will obviously do much not only to produce quality crops, but play a small part in preserving the environment.

Many of the cropping procedures and the economic issues in this book will equally apply under intensive organic gardening, with the tremendous advantage of bringing a superlative end-product for sale at greatly enhanced prices.

WEED CONTROL

Perhaps no aspect of horticulture has made more rapid progress than weed control in the last ten years or so. The high cost of labour has necessitated a very intensive programme of research into ways and means of controlling weeds, particularly on a selective basis between crops.

We do not intend to argue for or against the ethics of weed control and link this with environmental factors, as we fully believe that weedkillers are a necessary part of modern crop production and that, intelligently used according to directions, they are unlikely to give rise to long-term pollution problems. Chemical fertilisers are in much the same category, the emphasis being on their *intelligent* utilisation when and where required. One main principle is absolutely clear concerning weed control: to apply weedkillers accurately and affectively with good-quality apparatus. To apply a highly sophisticated weedkiller in a haphazard manner with a watering-can is like performing a delicate operation on a human being with a rusty gardening knife.

The economic benefits following the use of weedkillers are so enormous that they are almost unbelievable. A few acres of rose bushes manually weeded can run into hundreds of pounds for the cost of labour compared to a few pounds for Simazine, the same being true of weed-control work with many shrubs and fruit bushes. Paraquat and diquat based weedkillers, used in an intelligent way, can reduce weeding costs to a small fraction of what they would be with a hoe and the fingers.

Gardeners in the UK are strongly advised to study an up to date copy of the Agricultural Chemicals Scheme *Approved Products for the Farmer and Grower,* in addition to the *Weed Control Handbook* issued at regular intervals by the Weed Control Council. It is important to understand the basic principles under which weedkillers operate, bearing in mind that some weedkillers have more than one mode of action.

Soil-acting Weedkillers

These dissolve in the soil, the plant being killed by absorption of the weedkiller through its roots. Examples are Atrazine (Weedex A50 and others) (which is also contact—see page 61), Dichlobenol (Casoron G), Simazine (soil-acting, several formulations) and sodium chlorate (which is also a translocated material—see below). The main use of these soil-acting chemicals is either for cleaning-up land initially, prior to cultivation, or, in the case of some such as Dichlobenol and Simazine, for selective control in fruit or shrubs.

Some soil-acting herbicides are so persistent that they can only be used for ground which is not intended for cropping for a long time or for driveways, paths, etc, this being of particular interest for sales areas concerned with garden centres or roadside stalls. Care must be taken with sodium chlorate, which is extremely soluble and liable to 'creep'; it must not be applied anywhere close to crops. It is also highly inflammable under certain circumstances, especially where it has dissolved and dried on grass or herbage.

The economic implications of cleaning land chemically with soil-acting herbicides are far-reaching to the extreme and it is important that they be given intelligent consideration in any situation involving land reclamation.

Translocated Herbicides
These are absorbed by roots or foliage and transported throughout the plant; examples are most of the hormone weedkillers, for selective weed control in turf, and couch-grass-controlling herbicides such as Aminotriazole. These have a vital role to play in the control of deep-rooted weeds, especially in plantations of fruit, either separately, or by applying in combination with other translocated herbicides such as paraquat—which although it is translocated acts as a contact weedkiller (see below).

Contact Weedkillers
These kill when the chemical ultimately destroys the leaf tissue. Material such as sulphate of iron which kills moss in turf is typical of contact weedkillers, although the translocated weedkillers paraquat and diquat also act as contact weed-killers, almost like a chemical flame-gun. Contact weedkillers have a vital role to play for pre-emergence use or inter-row application.

Selective Weed Control

Some understanding of the role of selective weedkillers for any aspect of commercial crop production is essential. Whether weedkillers are soil-acting, translocated, contact, or a mixture of two or more types, it is important to realise that their selective use where 'weeds' are killed and the 'crop' is left intact is possible due to a variety of circumstances. Possibly the simplest example is where a soluble yet *total* weedkiller such as Simazine is used between shrubs and roses or on fruit crops. What actually happens is that the Simazine remains as a slowly dissolving surface skin, killing newly germinated or young weeds on the surface. The Simazine, at the application rates recommended, does not penetrate to the root area of the 'crop'. Botanical selection also enters into things to a certain extent; some weedkillers are harmful to one botanical group and not to another. Even Simazine has relatively little effect against members of the Polygonaceae family, to which several obnoxious weeds belong. Blackcurrant seedlings develop freely in Simazine-treated areas between the bushes and there are numerous examples of this sort of situation. Botanical selectivity is put to good use in vegetable crops, whereby a crop of lettuce belonging to the Compositae family and treated with CIPC (chlorpropham) is unaffected, whereas other botanical groups of weeds are killed. In time, unfortunately, a predominance of composite weeds develops.

Important Note

Remember with weedkillers that it is the quantity of active ingredient applied to a given area, not the quantity of water in which it is dissolved, which is vital. Spraying appliances may be high or low volume, and the total quantity of diluted spray applied to a given area, and how much spray material it contains, should be calculated. With either manual or mechanised sprayers the output per given period of time *must be obtained from the manufacturer* when the time taken to cover a certain area of ground is taken into account.

ARTIFICIAL LIGHT

The application of artificial light to various growth processes has developed very considerably in recent years. They have a practical and vital part to play in many facets of commercial culture. But the techniques should be properly evaluated in economic terms before being adopted.

Basically speaking there are four main applications for the use of artificial light:

1. *Light for working convenience*: to extend the length of day during the shorter day periods, and required as a matter of course by most serious gardeners, at least in northern latitudes. Ordinary tungsten filament or fluorescent-tube lighting to acceptable level is satisfactory, if the lights are so installed that they avoid working shadows.

2. *Supplementary lighting*: this involves the use of high-intensity lighting to supplement the natural daylight. It is a technique used for the propagation stage of tomatoes, cucumbers, chrysanthemums at a young stage, and countless other applications. Deciding which form of lighting to use has been the subject of some experimentation in recent years. HLRG or MBFRU lamps have been used in recent years, in general about 2½–3ft above the bench where the plants are being treated. Still more recently fluorescent tubes backed by reflector boards have been used, although this method arouses some controversy as natural light is largely excluded.

The economic issues surrounding the use of supplementary lighting are not clear cut, yet it can be said from carefully conducted trials and working experience on many holdings that the propagating period needed for many plants in poor light areas can be shortened, in the case of tomatoes by some 2–3 weeks; and also that it is possible to produce better-balanced plants, irrespective of natural light levels, which usually perform better when planted, at least initially. This can give savings in both heating bills and space. It seems likely that light-meters may become an accepted part of supplementary lighting systems, so that they switch on only when natural light falls below an acceptable level.

Further sources of light, such as sodium (SOX), are also being tried out, but as yet are not generally in use.

3. *'Growing Rooms'*: Artificial light has been used to produce crops in daylight-excluded buildings of high thermal insulation for a considerable number of years. It was first adopted commercially when low-intensity lighting was used to bring bulbs such as tulips, hyacinths and daffodils into flower. It should be noted that the only warmth required is the waste heat from the light, and obviously there is considerable economic advantage in the technique.

It was also discovered a great many years ago that high-intensity artificial light could readily substitute for natural light, provided the right spectrum of light was employed.

Small 'growing cabinets' using a high level of lighting to replace natural light, but of limited capacity, have been used for many years by research workers anxious to carry out botanical research over the full year irrespective of season. These units were, in the main, highly sophisticated and could be controlled within fine temperature limits as they had heating and refrigeration units installed. The high cost involved in making larger-capacity units of similar design for commercial usage was recently appraised, resulting in the development of the real commercial growing room, which although relatively costly was economically feasible. Many of these growing rooms were installed in commercial nurseries, being used initially for bedding-plant production and later for a wide variety of propagation, including tomatoes. Still more recently various adaptations of growing rooms involving less capital expense have been developed, including those in plastic greenhouses used for 'programmed' lettuce and tomato production.

The main advantage of a growing room in any form is the ability to provide 'standard' growing conditions irrespective of outside weather or time of year. One can plan crop production on a precise basis, and in most cases considerably shorten the propagation period, especially for plants such as lettuce and the majority of bedding plants which can be given twenty-four hours continuous light.

The economic implications are once again unclear, due largely to the changing techniques which have occurred, yet accurate costings on lettuce and tomato propagation (see appendix) do show considerable advantages. Care must be taken when making economic comparisons in this sphere to allow for capital investment.

4. *Daylight Manipulation and Night-break Techniques*: The physiological processes involved in crop production are diverse to the extreme, yet a number of plants of considerable economic importance, such as mid- and late-flowering chrysanthemums, will only initiate their flower buds when the day length is between about $12\frac{1}{2}$–$13\frac{1}{2}$ hours. Year-round culture of such plants has become possible due to the use of lighting techniques, largely on a low-intensity basis (for chrysanthemums at any rate) and shading during the naturally long days.

Many other plants can also benefit from what are called 'night-break' techniques, whereby light is given in the middle of the night for periods of around two hours, in this case using high-intensity lighting. Economic benefits are considerable, as high-quality items can be produced earlier.

CARBON DIOXIDE ENRICHMENT

Green plants must have a supply of CO_2 (carbon dioxide) if they are to carry out the vital process of photosynthesis.

Carbon dioxide is available in the atmosphere at approximately 300 parts per million, and research over many years in glasshouse culture has shown that there are times when the rate or form in which plants grow may be restricted by the natural limit of carbon dioxide, usually in periods of high light and rapid growth. The atmosphere of the greenhouse can be enriched with additional carbon dioxide in several ways: Burning natural gas, paraffin or propane (propane being preferable to paraffin as it contains less sulphur), the use of liquid CO_2 from a bulk tank dispersed through polythene pipes, or dry ice, which is solidified CO_2. All these methods are used commercially, yet while there is much evidence to show that the extra cost of giving CO_2 is justified in producing certain better quality or earlier crops, there is also doubt in certain quarters about just how this works.

Early tomato growers invariably use additional carbon dioxide, at both the propagating and early growth stages, and it appears to result in a more balanced plant which produces bigger and earlier bottom trusses of fruit. With flower crops there are many instances where quality has been much improved with carbon dioxide.

It must be appreciated, however, that its use does not cancel out the need for good husbandry; indeed it could well be that the reverse is the case and that good husbandry is the first essential, the carbon dioxide further improving yields, quality and earliness.

The exact techniques for the use of carbon dioxide are readily available from horticultural advisers, fuel or carbon dioxide suppliers.

PEST AND DISEASE CONTROL

While considerable advances have been made in the control of pests and diseases, many problems still remain. Indeed the resistance which many pests have developed to chemicals is

Page 67 (*above*) Rock gardening can be aesthetically satisfying and is a 'shop window' for potential customers seeking to clothe their own rock gardens at home; (*below*) black polythene mulching has many roles. Here it is being used for strawberries to cut down weeding and prevent damage to fruit from soil splash.

Page 68 (above) The polythene bag system of tomato culture is excellent for 'played out' or 'sick' soil. It also allows the greenhouse to be used for other purposes before placing the tomatoes in their growing positions at a more advanced stage of growth; (below) tomatoes always enjoy a ready sale in both small and large amounts, but to be commercially rewarding cropping must be at a high level and quality first class.

causing grave concern. There has, however, in recent years been something of a 'breakthrough' with systemic disease-controlling chemicals such as 'Benlate'. Plant breeders have also now introduced resistance to many diseases into many species of plants (eg tomatoes), which are listed in any seeds-man's catalogue.

SOIL STERILISATION

In addition to established methods of soil sterilisation by heat, there is increasing use of chemical sterilisers (see page 60).

GROWING MEDIA FOR CROPS

Considerable changes in philosophy concerning the media in which plants are grown have taken place during the last decade and it seems that further changes are inevitable, dictated by economic and other factors. This is more the case with plants being grown under glass, where monocultural (repeated culture of the same or similar crops in the same soil) problems are likely to arise, and there is increasing difficulty in obtaining replacement soil, or alternatively high cost in sterilising the existing soil (see page 206).

Where plants are being grown and sold with the growing medium, which includes pot plants, bedding plants, containerised shrubs and young plants such as tomatoes, carnations and others, there has been great emphasis on 'standardisation', necessitating a growing medium other than soil, as the latter, apart from requiring sterilisation, varies considerably in texture and nutritional standards. Weight is also a factor of importance. The classical work of W. J. C. Lawrence and A. P. Newell in the 1930s laid the foundation for a whole new approach to growing media and succeeded in initiating set standards which if adhered to, would ensure a high qual-

E

ity plant; and at one fell swoop they did away with the need for those countless different formulations, many of them 'secret', which gardeners and growers at that time were prone to use.

The passage of time and the high cost of labour, while not ousting the famous John Innes formulae completely, have brought a widespread swing to soil-less media based largely on peat and peat/sand formulae which originated at the University of California, and more recently on peat/synthetic materials.

Soils and growing media based principally on peat have received tremendous publicity in recent years and include growing systems for crops such as tomatoes which are now an accepted part of commercial culture. We are already on the threshold of synthetic composts and simple hydroponics, the use of nutrient solutions, which could, in time, take over from peat-based media. Systems concerned with lignite and other media of high capillarity, are showing great possibilities.

It had been thought for a great many years that soil, charged as it is with countless billions of micro-organisms, was an essential constituent for all growing media. This in fact is true where compound fertilisers which depend on micro-organisms to break them down to simple soluble elements capable of being absorbed by the plants are to be used. It has, however, been known for a good many years that plants supplied with initially soluble and palatable nutrients can grow well without any micro-organic activity. Inert aggregates such as sand or gravel are introduced merely as 'holding' media for the plant roots, and the plants are fed on a nutrient solution. An examination of any form of culture shows that plants are in fact ultimately growing in nutrient solution anyway, the soil and its micro-organisms carrying out the function of rendering the nutrients soluble to the plants.

Provided there can be an intelligent appreciation of the need for constant 'topping up' of the nutrients in soil-less mixes, compared to relying on the longer-term availability of nutrients in a soil-derived compost, excellent results can be achieved. This means quite simply the use of liquid feeds on a constant basis. It must also be appreciated that nutritional deficiencies and unbalance can much more readily occur in soil-less mixes due to the lack of the 'buffering' which is provided by soil-based media.

The economic consequences of using soil-less media bought ready to use, either for pot or crop culture, can only be taken in true context by weighing up the actual cost of the product, and the saving of the labour and lack of what would be needed for self-mixing composts against the results.

CHAPTER 8

Taxation

Apart from the normal taxation of the profits from a full-time enterprise, any additional income from a garden or part-time holding will also be liable to tax. The aim of this chapter is to indicate how to keep tax to an absolute minimum.

One is entitled to deduct from gross returns all expenses incurred in growing and selling crops. A simple account-book to record all receipts and payments made during the year is well worthwhile. Neglecting to deduct £10 spent on fertilisers will mean about £3 extra tax (assuming tax is being paid at the standard rate). All sales notes and receipted payment vouchers should be carefully filed away until the tax inspector has agreed to the tax return. This is necessary, since he may demand evidence that certain payments have been made.

In addition to the more obvious expenses of the growing of the crop, there are a number of other items which may be charged. This is because of the difference in tax regulations between an employee and someone who is self-employed, even on a part-time basis. Here is a check list of some items:

1. *Payments to wife or other members of the family*
If the family help in any way with the growing of the crop, selling produce at the door, keeping the records and accounts of the business, wages can be paid for the work done. The wage charge must be based on current rates paid for the type of work. An inflated claim will simply be disallowed by the tax inspector and may even make him suspicious of other claims, however legitimate these may be.

Similarly if the children help with the fruit picking or weeding they can be paid a wage. An important point is that all wages charged must be actually paid, but no regulation states how the money paid in wages should be used. In 1973, for example, a wife could be paid up to £325 per year and children up to £115 without tax having to be paid.

2. *Tools, repairs and depreciation*

The cost of tools, the repair, upkeep and depreciation of equipment, glasshouses, frames, roads and fences may be wholly or partly deducted as business expenses. The cost of any tools, repairs or maintenance incurred during the year can be charged in full. In the case of large items such as a new glasshouse, used for business purposes, depreciation at $\frac{1}{10}$th of the cost can be charged against profits. Depreciation on general machinery and equipment can be charged at 15 per cent of the original cost (or written-down value) each year; thus a machine costing £100 would be depreciated as follows:

Year 1	Cost of machine	£100
	Less Depreciation @ 15%	15
	Written-down value	£ 85
Year 2	Written-down value at start	85
	Less Depreciation @ 15%	13
	Written-down value at end	£ 72

3. *Car expenses*

The cost of running a car to transport produce to market, or to collect materials needed for the business, is entitled to be charged. This includes not only petrol and oil but also a share of repair costs, road tax, insurance and depreciation. Depreciation on cars is usually allowed at 25 per cent of the original cost or written-down value and the charge is calculated as shown in the previous section. A check should be kept on the mileage covered for business purposes, so that a proper share of these expenses can be charged.

4. *Use of facilities in the house*

If a room of the house is used as an office or for plant raising, a proportion of house maintenance may be charged. This includes a share of rates, rent, insurance, repairs and upkeep of house and furnishings, heat and light. Telephone calls for business can also be charged. Again the need for these facilities and the share of the cost charged must be justified.

Each year a tax assessment form will be sent from the Inland Revenue for the year ended 5 April. On this form any additional income must be declared. To do this, a profit statement should be prepared showing the profit earned after deducting all legitimate expenses. This should be prepared from a summary of revenue and expenditure recorded in the account book.

An example illustrating the layout of a profit statement follows. If in any doubt, further information and advice should be sought from a tax accountant.

PROFIT STATEMENT FOR YEAR ENDED 5 APRIL 197–

Revenue from Sales

Vegetables	£75	
Fruit	30	
Shrubs	65	
Bedding Plants	50	£220

Less Expenditure:

Seed, plants, etc	45	
Car expenses—$\frac{1}{10}$th share	25	
Telephone—$\frac{1}{4}$ share	6	
House rates, etc—$\frac{1}{6}$th share	14	
Tools, repairs, etc	5	
Wages—wife—150 hours @ 30p	45	
Depreciation of Glasshouse—$\frac{1}{10}$th	15	£155
Net Profit		£ 65

VALUE ADDED TAX

Anyone running a business and producing goods or services to a value of £5,000 per annum or more must register with, and make periodic returns of VAT, to HM Customs & Excise. Food products are zero-rated and therefore do not bear any tax, but this does not mean that growers wholly or mainly engaged in food production do not have to register. Indeed it is in their own interests to do so, even though they will be reclaiming tax paid on their purchases rather than paying it on sales. Because of this, growers producing zero-rated goods who have a turnover of less than £5,000 per annum should apply for voluntary registration.

Ornamental crops such as flowers, pot plants and shrubs are liable for tax at the standard rate (10 per cent at the time of writing). It could therefore be in the interests of garden-centre owners and other nurseries producing ornamental crops not to register if their turnover is under the £5,000 limit.

Tax invoices will be received from suppliers showing the amount of VAT paid on purchases. Similarly tax invoices must be supplied to customers (other than consumers) showing the VAT collected on sales. Direct retail sales to the public should include VAT and the gross takings must be recorded daily. All transactions should be recorded and the tax invoices filed. These records will provide the basis for preparing a tax account and completing the return (form VAT100) for each tax period. Growers producing and selling standard-rated items will make returns every quarter, while producers of zero-rated items who are reclaiming tax can apply to make returns monthly.

EXAMPLE OF VAT ACCOUNT FOR APRIL–JUNE 197–

Tax due

output tax on sales (wholesale) of £22,000	£2,000
output tax on sales (retail) 1/11th of daily takings, say	300
output tax on credit sales (not wholesale)	100
	£2,400

Deductible input tax

input tax on purchases	1,400
	£1,000

Add under payments of VAT with respect to

previous periods	100
Net Tax Due	£1,100

CHAPTER 9

Marketing

In the UK, horticultural produce in bulk is traditionally disposed of through wholesale markets which are to be found in many of the towns and cities near the main production centres. On delivery by the grower, the produce is sold by brokers or salesmen who charge porterage and commission (usually 10 per cent) for performing this service. Proper grading and presentation are essential if reasonable prices are to be obtained. There are now standard grades for many crops, which are enforced by Ministry of Agriculture inspectors (Department of Agriculture in Scotland) and further grades to conform to EEC standards are certain for the future. Growers must make themselves familiar with the size and descriptive grades for these crops, on which leaflets can be obtained from their respective authorities. One problem with wholesale marketing within the European framework is the vast fluctuation in price structure which can occur, especially in periods of glut, so that the system frequently comes under severe criticism. It is usually found that there are considerable price variations from region to region, which suggests that the problem is mainly one of communication and distribution.

Selling direct to shops is only a worthwhile alternative if it is possible to provide a regular supply of produce, well graded and packaged. Few shopkeepers are likely to be interested in an irregular supply of produce of variable quality. Some shops prefer to feature local produce for which they are often able to charge a premium price. They may also be interested in 'home-made' jams and preserves and an approach could be made to local shops with some samples. Again presentation and particularly wholesome appearance are of vital importance. The prices a shopkeeper will pay are usually broadly based on those in the wholesale market, but do tend to be higher for consistent quality. There is the saving in commission charges and perhaps also in carriage if the shopkeeper picks up at the nursery.

In recent years there have been some dramatic changes in the methods of retailing, the most important of which has been the rise of the large 'cut-price' selling organisations such as supermarkets, discount stores and more recently the frozen-food distributors who can offer substantial discounts to customers with deep freezes who are prepared to buy in large quantities. One of the problems is that individual growers find it difficult to provide the volume of supplies which these large retail outlets require. Even the wholesale markets have failed to provide the volume of consistent quality and grade of produce which the retailer needs, causing them, in the UK, to turn to co-operative organisations in the Channel Islands or the Continent. Obviously what is required in the UK on a wide front is a reorganisation of supplies either within the wholesale market itself or by a group of growers acting together to meet the needs of these new outlets. The co-operatives that do exist in the UK still handle only a fraction of the total output of the country.

There seems little doubt that supermarkets and other large retail outlets will command the largest share of the market for fruit and vegetables (whether fresh or frozen) in the future, largely for the reason that they offer such tremendous 'one-stop' advantages for shoppers. On the ornamental side too the supermarket provides an opportunity of exposing the more luxury items to a mass consumer market. Bedding plants and pot plants, for instance, have been sold in supermarkets with enormous success. It must be emphasised that in some cases success depends on bringing the price down to a very competitive level, so that it is only worthwhile for the grower who is looking for volume of sales rather than a high margin of profit on each item.

A more usual way of selling bedding plants and shrubs is by advertising in the local paper and selling direct to the consumer. Mail orders can also be obtained by advertising in papers and magazines with a wide circulation, but recent increases in transport costs have tended to make this outlet less lucrative.

Direct sales to the consumer can be worthwhile if properly organised. Indeed a grower can often make more money selling a crop than he can by growing it. Constant interruption of the production routine must, however, be avoided; this kind of selling can be more expensive than it seems. The retail side should be organised as a separate section with its own sales staff. This may be simply a part-time assistant or a full-time selling organisation.

For the nursery or garden situated on a main road, a roadside stall can sell produce direct to passing motorists. (Before doing this, however, it is necessary to check with the local authority and to obtain planning permission.) Retail selling units on a larger scale have also been developed, the garden centre being the outstanding example. Garden centres are excellent venues for sales-promotion drives, featuring items in season, but demand high investment.

SUMMARY OF SELLING METHODS

1. Wholesale markets. Advantage: produce disposed of in bulk, with minimum time involvement. Disadvantages: fluctuation in price structure and commission charges.

2. Direct to shops. Advantages: savings in commission and carriage. Disadvantage: regular supply of produce essential.

3. Supermarkets. Advantage: opportunity to present new

products. Disadvantages: big volume of supplies required. Very competitive prices.

4. Advertising in local paper. Advantage: excellent for attracting local interest. Disadvantage: usually means considerable time involvement in selling what may be relatively small amounts of produce—see Direct selling.

5. Mail order. Advantage: convenient for customers over a wide area if ordering procedures are made simple. Disadvantage: ever-rising transport costs.

6. Direct selling. Advantages: no commission charges and top prices. Disadvantages: heavy time involvement, which can cut time available for producing crops, and selling can be a lot more expensive than it seems.

7. Garden centres. Advantage: if well laid-out can induce high sales. Disadvantages: high level of capital investment, and very seasonal unless all-the-year-round selling lines are incorporated.

PART II

Crop Guide
Cultural Programmes
Costs and Returns

IMPORTANT NOTE

Rapidly rising prices of oil and other materials must be taken into account when using these figures. A further complication is the devaluation of the pound in relation to imported material.

Vegetables

The growing of vegetables for household use is becoming increasingly popular, not only as a means of helping the household budget but to have quality and freshness available. So far as growing them for sale is concerned, there seems always to be an outlet for quality items.

In the following notes, the figures given for production costs and returns are based on large-scale growing and wholesale prices. Where small-scale growing is undertaken, and retail prices are received, the economic picture may be changed. Commercial vegetable growing is in fact increasingly in the hands of large-scale producers using mechanical equipment, including precision seed-sowers (small models of these are of course available), transplanters and various forms of mechanical harvesters.

There is increasing scope for the production of vegetables under plastic structures, but it is difficult to be precise here about yields and margins as so many variables are involved—including of course the initial cost and depreciation of the plastic structures in the first place.

Farmyard manure costs are not included here except where stated, as in many instances they should be shared among several crops grown on a particular site on a seasonal or rotational basis.

On pest and disease control, brief recommendations are given for convenience, and readers are advised to consult an up-to-date copy of the Agricultural Chemicals Approval Scheme booklet *Approved Products for Farmers and Growers*. Again, costs of weed control are included, but the above booklet will also be useful here, and so will the Ministry of Agriculture Short Term leaflets which give up-to-date details.

ASPARAGUS

A crop which tends to be grown on a specialised basis, especially for canning.

Culture: Permanent bed.

Cultivation: Dig or plough deep in a position well exposed to sun. Soil in very sticky condition should be treated with ashes, sand or manure/compost at 25 tons per acre (1cwt per 10sq yd).

Lime: to pH 5.6–5.8.

Fertiliser: Bonemeal at 2½oz per yard of row (4cwt per acre) in open trench.

Plant: 2-year roots in April (later in cold areas). Seeds should be sown in late March in slightly heated greenhouse, 24 seeds per box, or in May out of doors in drills 12in apart and 1in deep. Transplant young plants 12–15in apart and leave for two years until they flower to indicate male plants which are more productive. In cropping areas dig or plough out a trench 6–7in deep and plant 15–18in apart, leaving 4ft between trenches. Half-fill the trench with soil until growth begins. At the end of each growing season remove decayed growth by cutting, and the following spring treat with manure mulch before ridging the ground slightly. It is also desirable to treat with a general fertiliser at the rate of 2–3oz per sq yd (6cwt per acre) and this can be done in April. Simazine-based weed-killers are normally used.

Harvest: Cut the tips poking through the soil with a sharp knife, commencing third week of June in warmer areas, such as Southern England, and early/mid July in cooler areas.

This vegetable is sometimes attacked by the asparagus beetle, so dust with BHC early in May. Should the plants develop a rusty appearance they should be sprayed with Dithane.

Life of crop: 10 years, of which 8 years are cropping.

Target yields: (10-year average): 30cwt per acre.

Packaging: Lettuce crates, 20 bundles per crate—2,240 bundles × 1½lbs.

Crop costs and returns per acre

Revenue—2,240 bundles @ 45p	£608	
Less commission—approx 10%	61	
Less crop expenses:		£547
Seed—2lb @ £1.50 (over 10 years)		0.3
Manure—25 tons (home-produced, over 10 years)		1.3
Fertiliser—6cwt compound @ £2		12.0
Sprays—as required (weedkillers, insecticides)		4.0
Packaging—112 crates @ 8.5p		9.5
Carriage—112 crates @ 5p		5.6
		£32.7

Margin per acre: £514

Labour requirement (average over 10 years): 447 hours, heaviest months May and June (182 hours each).

Margin per hour worked: £1.10

BEANS (FRENCH)

A crop with a limited but constant market.

Culture: suitable for culture in plastic structures, especially climbing varieties. Classed as root crop. There are two types —dwarf and climbing. The former is more popular as it requires no support; not a crop for cold districts.

Seed: on a small scale ½ pint per 100ft single row, 84lb per acre on large scale.

Cultivation: digging and ploughing with manure at 1cwt per 10sq yd, or 25 tons per acre, when necessary.

F

Fertilisers: 1¾oz per sq yd or 4cwt per acre.

Sowing: late April (warmer areas) and early May (cooler areas), or on a smaller scale in a greenhouse in boxes in April. Outdoors sow the seeds 2–4in apart, in rows 18–24in apart.

Acclimatise greenhouse-sown seed to outside conditions for late May-early June planting out. Cloches can advance sowing/planting date by 14–20 days. Position cloches ten days before planting. Thin out to leave seedlings 6–8in apart finally. (Climbing French beans can also be grown in greenhouses if sown with heat in March/April in rows 2–3ft apart.)

Cultivation in season: regular hoeing and allow no summer drying out. Support climbing beans with string nets 6ft high or bean poles. If the ground is moist enough give extra feeding with nitro-chalk at 1oz per sq yd or 2cwt per acre when the pods swell.

Harvest: pick the beans when fairly young and store surplus crop in salt or allow pods to dry, extract seeds and use as haricots (white beans).

Problems: flower-dropping (from variation in temperature). Water crop and mulch with peat, spent hops or grass cuttings (if untreated with hormone weed-killer).

Target yield: 2½ tons per acre = 700 boxes × 8lb.

Packaging: cardboard boxes—8lb per box.

Crop costs and returns per acre

Revenue—5,600lb @ 5p	£280	
Less commission @ 10%	28	
	——	£252
Less crop expenses:		
Seed—84lb @ 27p		23
Fertiliser—4cwt compound @ £2.7		11
2cwt nitro-chalk @ £2.5		5
Sprays—as required		4
Packaging—700 @ 5p		35
Carriage—700 @ 4p		28
		——
		£106

Margin per acre: £146 (can be much higher for protected crop).
Labour requirement: 270 hours, heaviest months May (40 hours) and July (180 hours).

Margin per hour worked: £0.54

BEANS (RUNNER)

Can be a considerable demand in certain areas. The culture and economics of runner beans are basically similar to French beans; they are sown in May, or in pots or soil blocks under glass in April, and planted out in early June. Seed requirements are ½lb per 80–100ft row (60lb per acre). Can be trained on 8–10ft poles arranged as tripods, sowing or planting two plants at the base of each pole, or sow or plant 6–8in apart in rows 6ft apart. Not a crop for cold districts.
Target yield: 5 tons per acre—1,400 boxes × 8lb.
Packaging: cardboard boxes—8lb per box.

Crop costs and returns per acre

Revenue—11,200lb @ 5p	£560	
Less commission @ 10%	56	
		£504
Less crop expenses:		
Seed—60lb @ 30p		18
Fertiliser—4cwt compound @ £2.7		11
2cwt nitro-chalk @ £2.5		5
Sprays—as required		4
Packaging—1,400 @ 5p		70
Carriage—1,400 @ 4p		56
		£164

Margin per acre: £340
Labour requirement: 615 hours, heaviest months August (140 hours) and April (110 hours).

Margin per hour worked: £0.55

BEETROOT

An important root crop for bunching and boiling.

Culture: a very suitable crop for plastic structures.

Seed requirements: 1oz per 100ft. 10–16lb per acre. No manure applications. Good deep cultivation.

Lime: to pH 6–6.4

Fertiliser: 3–4oz per square yard—8–9cwt per acre.

Sowing: sow seed in late April/May/June in drills ½in deep and 18–24in apart, or sow seed in groups 4–5in apart, using 'monogerm' seed. Cloches can be used for early crops. Thin out globes to 4–5in apart or allow much closer spacing for bunching; long and intermediate to 6–8in apart.

Seasonal cultivation: top dress with nitrate of soda at ½oz per square yard (1cwt per acre) after thinning. Hoe regularly. Spray for greenfly. Market in bunches or bags.

Target yield: 14 tons/acre or 1,120 bags.

Packaging: net bags—28lb/bag.

Crop costs and returns per acre

Revenue—1,120 @ 30p	£336	
Less commission @ 10%	34	
Less crop expenses:	——	£302
Seed—12lb @ £1.50		18
Fertiliser—9cwt compound @ £2.7		24
1cwt @ £1		1
Sprays—as required		5
Packaging—1,120 bags @ 3p		34
Carriage—1,120 bags @ 5p		56
		£138

Margin per acre: £164 (can be higher for early crops).
Labour requirement: 303 hours, highest months July (150 hours) and June (72 hours).

Margin per hour worked: £0.59

BRUSSELS SPROUTS

Constant demand in winter months for quality item, but difficult to compete with large-scale producers using mechanical strippers. Cabbage family.

Seed: ⅛oz for transplanting 100–150 plants, ½lb for transplanting 1 acre, direct drilling 3lb per acre.
Culture: good, well drained land.
Lime: to pH 6·5–6·8
Fertiliser: 2oz per sq yd (5cwt/acre).
Sowing: sow early crops in cold frames in March, second early in seed bed in April, for planting May/June at 2–2½ft apart or more, according to variety. Direct drilling at same density in April (can be wasteful of seed).
Seasonal cultivation: hoe regularly and top dress with nitrogen if slow growth. Puddle in BHC or similar for root fly, calomel for club-root at planting time. Spray for caterpillars and any other pests.
Target yield: 4 tons per acre or 448 nets × 20lb.
Packaging: nets—20lb.

Crop costs and returns per acre

Revenue—448 nets @ 50p	£224	
Less commission @ 10%	22	
Less crop expenses:	——	£202
Seed—3lb @ £10		30
Fertiliser—8cwt compound @ £3		24
Sprays—as required		9
Packaging—448 nets @ 3p		13
Carriage—448 nets @ 4p		18
		——
		£94

Margin per acre: £108

Labour requirement: 227 hours, highest months December (63 hours) and November (36 hours). But labour variable according to cultural system.

Margin per hour worked: £0.51

CARROTS (main-crop)

Root crop. Tend to be grown on a large scale on contract.
Seed: ½oz per 100ft row (4–6lb per acre). Pelleted seed 20lb per acre.
Cultivation: good light land. Fresh manure not advised.
Lime: to pH 6·3–6·4.
Fertiliser: 2oz per sq yd (5cwt/acre) before sowing in drills ½in deep in April/May at 12–24in apart, or 4–5 row raised beds on field scale. Use BHC for carrot fly (or obtain dressed seed).
Target yield: 15 tons per acre.
Packaging: nets—28lb.

Crop costs and returns per acre (main-crop)

Revenue—15 tons @ £18		£270	
Less commission @ 10%		27	
			£243
Less crop expenses:			
Seed—4lb @ £1			4
Fertiliser—5cwt compound @ £2.4			12
Sprays—as required			8
Packaging—1,200 nets @ 3p			36
Carriage—1,200 @ 5p			60
			£120

Margin per acre: £123

Labour requirement: 202 hours, heaviest months November (39 hours) and October and December (38 hours).

Margin per hour worked: £0.61

Bunched carrots
Bunched carrots can be grown on similar lines, either in frames or under cloches, sowing in March or early April or in succession thereafter out of doors. They can be sown broadcast in frames and drills, or 2–3in apart under cloches. Yields

and returns can be a good deal higher than for main-crop carrots. An ideal crop for plastic structures.

CAULIFLOWER (Early crop, transplanted)

Tends to be grown on a large scale as a field crop.

Culture: cabbage family; a rotated crop. Grow to maturity in succession and not glut, by choice of varieties.

Seed: ½oz produces 100 plants on small scale, or ¼lb per acre for transplanting.

Cultivation: rich land is necessary and should be dug or ploughed well, early enough to allow settling. When soil is poor apply farmyard manure at 1cwt per 10sq yd or 25 tons per acre. A well-drained open site is necessary and before planting land should be forked or rotavated lightly, then firmed with the feet or rolled.

Lime: to pH 6·5–6·7.

Fertiliser: general fertiliser at 2oz per sq yd (5cwt/acre) broadcast or close to planting area a few days before planting.

Sowing: seed can be broadcast or sown in drills 9in apart in a cold frame (or sown in blocks) in the previous September, or in boxes or blocks in heated greenhouses in February/ early March. *Culture of later crops*: for later crops seed can be broadcast or sown in drills ½in deep and 9in apart, or again in blocks, in a cold frame in mid-late March, or out of doors in drills 9in apart in mid-April for really late crops, including winter cauliflower or broccoli.

Plant: autumn-sown cauliflower in April/early May, 2ft × 18 in apart (early types). Plant later types 2ft × 2ft apart in May/June.

Cultivation: in season, regular hoeing is generally essential. A light dressing of nitro-chalk (1cwt/acre) should be given to induce rapid growth.

Harvest: as the curds form, turn in the outer leaves for protection. For whiptail (molybdenum deficiency), apply sodium molybdate.

Target yield: 9,000 head per acre.

Packaging: Lettuce crates (average 7 per crate, maybe 6, 8 or more).

Crop costs and returns per acre

Revenue—9,000 @ 5p	£450	
Less commission @ 10%	45	
		£405
Less crop expenses:		
Seed—⅛lb @ £16 per lb	2	
Fertiliser—4cwt compound @ £2.7	11	
1cwt nitro-chalk @ £2.4	2	
Sprays—as required	4	
Packaging—1,240 crates @ 8.5p	105	
Carriage—1,240 crates @ 5p	62	
	£186	

Margin per acre: £219

Cost of farmyard manure is generally spread over a period and is not usually included.

Labour requirement: 380 hours, heaviest months March (85 hours) and April (60 hours).

Margin per hour worked: £0.58

CAULIFLOWER (summer/autumn crops)

Culture: as given for early crop.

Target yield: 7,000 heads per acre.

Packaging: lettuce crates (average 7 per crate, may be 6, 8 or more).

Crop costs and returns per acre

Revenue—7,000 @ 4p	£280	
Less commission @ 10%	28	
		£252
Less crop expenses:		
Seed—⅛lb @ £16 per lb	2	
Fertiliser—4cwt compound @ £2.7	11	
1cwt nitro-chalk @ £2.4	2	
Sprays—as required	4	
Packaging—1,000 crates @ 8.5p	85	
Carriage—1,000 crates @ 5p	50	
		£154

Margin per acre: £98

Labour requirement, summer: 183 hours, heaviest months July (69 hours) and August (40 hours).

Labour requirement, autumn: 183 hours, heaviest months September (40 hours) and August (39 hours).

Margin per hour worked: £0.50

CAULIFLOWER—winter (broccoli)

Culture: already given.

Target yield: 5,000 head per acre.

Packaging: lettuce crates (average 7 per crate).

Crop costs and returns per acre

Revenue—5,000 @ 5p	£250	
Less commission @ 10%	25	
		£225
Less crop expenses:		
Seed—⅛lb @ £16	2	
Fertiliser—4cwt compound @ £2.7	11	
1cwt nitro-chalk @ £2.4	2	
Sprays—as required	4	
Packaging—715 crates @ 8·5p	61	
Carriage—715 crates @ 5p	36	
		£116

Margin per acre: £109
Labour requirement: 169 hours, heaviest months April and May
(50 hours each).
Margin per hour worked: £0.63

CELERY (self-blanching and blanching)

Can be a lucrative crop for good land in mild districts. Ideal
for plastic structures.

Culture: a specially prepared area is required for self-
blanching celery or it can be grouped with root crops on a
small scale.

Seed: 1/25th–1/30th oz will produce 100 plants under good
conditions (2oz seed per acre).

Cultivation: good land which has been well dug and dressed
with farmyard manure for a previous crop is essential,
especially for the blanching type. Dig or plough to a good
depth. The self-blanching type is ideal for vacant cold
frames after the raising of other seedlings, and for plastic
structures.

Lime: pH of 5·8–6 is required.

Fertiliser: general fertiliser at 4–5oz per sq yd, 10cwt per acre,
before planting.

Sowing: early crop in boxes in heated greenhouse in
January/February. The later crop in cold frames in March/
April. When handling is possible, prick out to a distance of
2in in 1in soil or peat blocks, or beds out of doors.

Plant: from late May in warmer areas to late June in cooler
areas for main crop. Self-blanching 10–12in apart each way
in an open border or cold frames; plant in plastic structures
in April. Blanching in trenches 12in apart down centre of
trench. Trenches should be 3–4ft apart. On a field scale plant
5–6in apart in rows 5ft apart. Plant requirement 22,000 per
acre.

Cultivation in season: constant watering, hoe self-blanching. For blanching type, earth up when plants are 1ft high, tying stems together with soft string on a small scale to prevent soil entering between the leaves. On a small scale liquid feed every 10–14 days, or dress with Nitram at 2–3 cwt per acre on a large scale.

Harvest: self-blanching when 12–15in tall. Blanching type when required and of sufficient size.

Pests, etc: carrot fly—use BHC dust after planting and again three weeks later; celery fly—spray with Malathion when first discovered. Leaf spot—spray with Bordeaux before planting and at 3–4 week intervals.

Target yield: 8,500 bundles (× 2).

Packaging: cardboard boxes (4 bundles per box).

Crop costs and returns per acre (self-blanching)

Revenue—17,000 @ 4p*	£680	
Less commission @ 10%	68	
		£612
Less crop expenses:		
Seed—3oz @ £1.8		5
Fertiliser—13cwt (10 + 3) @ £2.7		35
Sprays—as required		4
Packaging—2,125 @ 5p		106
Carriage—2,125 @ 4p		85
		£235

Margin per acre: £377

Labour requirement: 1,190 hours, heaviest months April (320 hours) and September (220 hours).

Margin per hour worked: £0.32. Timing varies considerably according to region and whether crop is grown under plastic structures or out of doors.

*Possibly much higher for earlier crops from plastic structures.

CELERY (main-crop)

Culture: similar to self-blanching.
Target yield: 8,500 bundles (× 2).
Packaging: cardboard boxes (4 bundles per box).

Crop costs and returns per acre

Revenue—17,000 @ $3\frac{1}{2}$p	£595	
Less commission @ 10%	60	
		£535
Less crop expenses:		
Seed—2oz @ £1.8	3	
Fertiliser—13cwt (10 + 3) @ £2.7	35	
Sprays—as required	4	
Packaging—2,125 @ 5p	106	
Carriage—2,125 @ 4p	85	
	£233	

Margin per acre: £302
Labour requirement: 748 hours, heaviest months December (170 hours) and November (110 hours).

Margin per hour worked: £0.40

LEEKS

A specialised crop demanding excellent land for weight of crop.
Culture: special bed or very good soil.
Seed: $\frac{1}{16}$oz produces 100 plants (or 2lb per acre).
Cultivation: deep digging, manure at 1cwt per 10sq yd or 25 tons per acre.
Lime: to pH 6–6.5.
Fertiliser: slow-acting general at 5–6oz per sq yd (13cwt per acre) before planting.
Sowing: on small scale sow thinly in fish boxes during January/February. Transfer seedlings into fish boxes (48 per

box) with John Innes potting compost. On a large scale sow in frame in February/March. Harden off to meet outside conditions. Seeding direct can be achieved in mild areas in March for small leeks.

Plant: mid-May (large) and mid-June (smaller) in drills 3in deep, 12–24in apart or make holes with steel dibber 7–8in deep, 9in and 1ft apart, and 12–16in between rows. Remove tops of leaves to 6in, trim roots to $\frac{1}{2}$–$\frac{3}{4}$in to facilitate planting.

Cultivation in season: hoe (do not push soil into holes). Nitro-chalk at 1oz per 6 plants (8cwt per acre) in June. Liquid feed every 10–14 days in July and August on a small scale.

Harvest: lift with a fork or plough out when large enough.

Pests, etc: seldom any trouble, but a troublesome crop.

Target yield: 10 tons per acre or 22,000lb.

Packaging: lettuce crates, 3lb bundles, 6 bundles per crate.

Crop costs and returns per acre

Revenue—22,000lb @ 3p		£660	
Less commission @ 10%		66	
Less crop expenses:			£594
Seed—2lb @ £6			12
Fertiliser—13cwt compound @ £2.7			35
8cwt nitro-chalk @ £2.4			19
Sprays—as required			4
Packaging—1,240 @ 8.5p			105
Carriage—1,240 @ 5p			62
			£237

Margin per acre: £357

Labour requirement (will vary according to procedure adopted): 519 hours, heaviest months May (108 hours), June (105 hours).

Margin per hour worked: £0.73

LETTUCE

One of the best vegetable crops to grow. Invariably in demand (see also chapter 3).

Culture: crops can be rotated. There are two types—cabbage and cos, which is crisper.

Seed: ½oz per 100ft row (2lb per acre), 1lb broadcast, 3lb direct. Pelleted seed 20lb per acre (12 × 4in).

Cultivation: dig or plough deeply for best results. For poor soil manure at 1cwt per 10sq yd (25 tons/acre). Open sunny position.

Lime: to pH 6·5–7.

Fertiliser: general, high nitrogen content at 4oz per sq yd (10cwt per acre) before sowing.

Sowing: late February/early March (mid-March in the North) at 2–3 week intervals until July/August in rows 12–18in apart and thin to 8in. For frame crops, sow broadcast from mid-January/early February in heated frames and mid-February in cold frames, planting 8 × 8in or 9 × 9in apart. For the early transplanted crop, plant out in March/April at 8 × 12–18in apart. For planting in September sow till mid-August. For the greenhouse crop (see page 124) grow all year in good light areas if temperature is 45°F (7·2°C) minimum. Soil or peat blocks and pelleted seed are much used now. Growing rooms are utilised for programmed production (see Electricity Council booklet). Plants must be acclimatised to outside conditions.

Cultivation in season: hoe or grub as necessary. Irrigate if dry.

Pests, etc: greenfly (distortion of young plants)—use Malathion. Leatherjackets and wireworms (eat roots)—use BHC. Botrytis and toe rot—use fungicidal dust. Mildew—use Dithane.

LETTUCE (summer)

Target yield: 20,000 per acre.
Packaging: lettuce crates, 18–24 per crate depending on size.

Crop costs and returns per acre

Revenue—20,000 @ 2p	£400	
Less commission @ 10%	40	
		£360
Less crop expenses:		
Seed—3lb @ £4.5	14	
Fertiliser—10cwt compound @ £2.7	27	
Sprays—as required	4	
Packaging—1,000 @ 8.5p	85	
Carriage—1,000 @ 5p	50	
		£180

Margin per acre: £180

Labour requirement (peak will vary according to timing):
218 hours, heaviest months May (66 hours), June (48 hours).
Margin per hour worked: £0.82

LETTUCE (early transplanted)

Target yield: 36,000 lettuce per acre.
Packaging: lettuce crates, 20 per crate.

Crop costs and returns per acre

Revenue—36,000 @ 3p	£1080	
Less commission @ 10%	108	
		£972
Less crop expenses:		
Seed—1lb @ £4.5	5	
Fertiliser—10cwt compound @ £2.7	27	
Sprays—as required	4	
Packaging—1,800 @ 8.5p	153	
Carriage—1,800 @ 5p	90	
		£279

Margin per acre: £693

Labour requirement: 554 hours, heaviest months January (101 hours), June (98 hours). (Mechanically made already seeded soil blocks are tremendously labour saving.)

Margin per hour worked: £1.23

See page 124 for glasshouse lettuce details.

ONIONS (main-crop)

Tend to be a large-scale field crop.

Culture: a crop for good, rich, well-cultivated land or special bed on a smaller scale.

Seed: 1oz per 100ft row (4lb per acre).

Cultivation: dig or plough deeply in autumn, applying farmyard manure as available.

Lime: to pH 6–6.3.

Sowing: sow seed in seed bed in mild areas in August in drills ½in deep and 12–15in apart for planting in April/May at 9 × 18in, or sow thinly in heat in January/February. Alternatively sow broadcast thinly in heated frames. Harden off for planting out at 9 × 18in in March/April. Can also be planted under cloches on smaller scale. For later crops sow direct in drills 18–30in apart in March/April and thin out, except for small pickling onions which are left 'thick'.

Target yield: 14 tons per acre.

Packaging: 56lb nets.

Crop costs and returns per acre

Revenue—560 bags @ £1	£560	
Less commission @ 10%	56	
		£504
Less crop expenses:		
Seed—4lb @ £3.5	14	
Fertiliser—6cwt compound @ £3	18	
Sprays—as required	8	
Packaging—560 nets @ 5p	28	
Carriage—560 nets @ 5p	28	
	£96	

Margin per acre: £408

Labour requirement (using machinery—harvester used): 198 hours, heaviest months December (160 hours), July and September (10 each).

Margin per hour worked: £2.08

SALAD ONIONS

Always in demand over a long period.

Culture: not generally rotated.

Seed: 8oz per 100ft (32lb per acre).

Cultivation: Really good land is necessary. Dig deep, preferably in autumn, and apply all manure/compost available. Finish cultivation in time to consolidate before spring.

Lime: to pH 6–6·3.

Fertiliser: Compound (High K) at 5oz per sq yd (13cwt per acre), 2cwt nitro-chalk in season.

Sowing: sow in succession in drills 18–30in apart from March until September (for overwintering).

Pests, etc: onion fly—dust with BHC before sowing. Leek-moth larvae (eat leaves)—use DDT dust. Mildew—use Dithane. White rot—use calomel dust when sowing (seldom troublesome with syboes).

Target yield: 5 tons per acre or 11,200lb.

Packaging: cardboard boxes, $\frac{1}{4}$–$\frac{1}{2}$lb bundles, 8lb per box.

G

Crop costs and returns per acre

Revenue—11,200 @ 6p	£672	
Less commission @ 10%	67	
Less crop expenses:		£605
Seed—32lb @ £1.9		61
Fertiliser—13cwt @ £3		39
2cwt nitro-chalk @ £2.4		5
Sprays—4 pints		
Chlorpropham @ 50p		2
Others as required		4
Packaging—1,400 @ 5p		70
Carriage—1,400 @ 4p		56
		£237

Margin per acre: £368

Labour requirement: 987 hours, heaviest months July (480 hours), June (323 hours). Labour peak will vary according to timing.

Margin per hour worked: £0.37

PARSLEY

Always in demand over a long period—but outlet can be limited.

Culture: classed as root crop. Rotated.

Seed: ¼oz per 100ft row (6lb per acre).

Cultivation: Deep digging, farmyard manure at 1cwt per 14–15sq yd (20 tons per acre).

Lime: to pH 6·5.

Fertiliser: general at 4–5oz per sq yd (11cwt per acre) before sowing.

Sowing: on small scale in heated greenhouses in February. Prick off 48 per fish box and harden off for setting out mid-April at 9 × 12in apart. Outside mid-late April in drills ¼in deep and 12–18in apart. Other sowings June–August for transplanting in frame in October.

Cultivation in season: regular hoeing, thin out seedlings to 4–8in apart. Occasional liquid feeding. For weed control see appendix.

Harvest: cut when required.

Pests, etc: carrot fly—use BHC dust after thinning out.

Target yield: 3 × 5,000lb per acre—15,000lb.

Packaging: cardboard boxes, 4lb per box.

Crop costs and returns per acre

Revenue—15,000lb @ 7p	£1,050	
Less commission @ 10%	105	
		£945
Less crop expenses:		
Seed—6lb @ £1.9		11
Fertiliser—11cwt compound @ £2.7		30
Sprays—as required		4
Packaging—3,800 @ 5p		190
Carriage—3,800 @ 4p		152
		£387

Margin per acre : £558

Labour requirement: 191 hours, heaviest months August (28 hours), June (26 hours), July (25 hours).

Margin per hour worked: £2.92

RADISH

A crop which can enjoy excellent demand—specially suitable for plastic structures.

Culture: classed mainly as surface crop and rotated with lettuce.

Seed: 1oz per 2–3sq yd or per 100ft row (25lb per acre; 50lb for broadcasting or thick sowing).

Cultivation: any well-cultivated area or vacant cold frame out of doors. Manure is unnecessary, provided soil is of good texture.

Lime: to pH 6·5.

Fertiliser: general, high in nitrogen, at 5–6oz per sq yd (11cwt per acre) raked in evenly before sowing.

Sowing: in heated frame or greenhouse late January/February. Cold frame late February/early March, then outdoors (in very sheltered spot for early sowings). Succession sowing throughout April–June. On field scale for seedling production broadcast and cover with thin layer of riddled soil. For direct sowing, firm with back of spade. Drills ½in deep and 12–18in apart.

Cultivation in season: hoeing or grubbing after harvest, fork and rake over for re-sowing. Before each sowing, dress land with lime at 3–4oz per sq yd (ground limestone if available) and general fertiliser at 2–3oz per sq yd.

Harvest: pull young roots when still extremely tender.

Target yield: 3,500doz bunches per acre.

Packaging: cardboard box, 12 bunches per box.

Crop costs and returns per acre

Revenue—3,500doz bunches @ 30p	£1,050	
Less commission @ 10%	105	
		£945
Less crop expenses:		
Seed—50lb @ £1	50	
Fertiliser—11cwt general @ £3	33	
Lime	5	
Packaging—300 boxes @ 5p	15	
Carriage—300 boxes @ 4p	12	
	£115	

Margin per acre: £830

Labour requirement: 345 hours, heaviest months May (120 hours), April (110 hours). Labour peak will vary according to timing.

Margin per hour worked: £2.40

RHUBARB

Tends to be a large-scale field crop. The forced crop is likely to be more attractive.

Culture: use well-drained land, manure at 1cwt per 9–10 sq yd (25 tons per acre).

Lime: to pH 5·8.

Fertiliser: none till growth is well advanced in April, then compound at 5oz per sq yd (8cwt per acre). Apply sulphate of ammonia around each clump, and repeat in 5–6 weeks.

Sowing: thinly in April or more generally by division. Lift mature crowns in autumn, taking younger outer portions, and plant 3–4ft apart each way.

Cultivation in season: hoeing. Apply Simazine for weed control.

Harvest: pull stalks when large enough.

Pests, etc: crown rot (kills crowns)—plant fresh stock on new site.

Target yield: 12 tons per acre—1,920 stone.

Packaging: lettuce crates, 1½ stone per crate.

Crop costs and returns per acre

Revenue—1,920 stone @ 30p	£576	
Less commission @ 10%	57	
		£519
Less crop expenses:		
Rhubarb crowns (est over 10 years)		30
Fertiliser—2cwt sulphate of ammonia @ £1.5		3
8cwt compound @ £2.6		21
Farmyard manure—10 tons @ £1.5		15
Sprays—as required		6
Packaging—1,280 @ 8.5p		109
Carriage—1,280 @ 5p		64
		£248

Margin per acre: £271

Labour requirement: 272 hours, heaviest months March (42 hours), November (40 hours).

Margin per hour worked: £1

See also Forced rhubarb (page 116).

TURNIP (early)

A useful crop on a limited scale for direct supply.

Culture: ideal for plastic structures.

Seed: ½oz per 100ft (4lb per acre).

Cultivation: well-cultivated land not freshly dressed with farmyard manure.

Lime: to pH 6·5–6·8.

Fertiliser: 2oz per sq yd (4–5cwt per acre).

Sowing: sow broadcast in frames in February, under cloches in March, and out of doors in March/April in drills ½in deep and 12–24in apart. Harvest when ready.

Target yield: 400doz bunches per acre.

Packaging: lettuce crates—4 bunches per crate.

Crop costs and returns per acre

Revenue—4,800 bunches @ 10p		£480	
Less commission @ 10%		48	
			£432
Less crop expenses:			
Seed—4lb @ £1.2			5
Fertiliser—4cwt compound @ £2.8			11
Sprays—as required			4
Packaging—1,200 crates @ 8.5p			102
Carriage—1,200 crates @ 5p			60
			£182

Margin per acre: £250

Labour requirement: 260 hours, heaviest months June (120 hours), May (90 hours).

Margin per hour worked: £0.96

Other Vegetable Crops

There are many other vegetable crops which, although useful for home supply, are not generally considered as being highly rewarding for sale, especially on a small scale, although they may well enjoy a specialist outlet. Some also useful for deep freezing.

ARTICHOKES (Jerusalem)

Lime: to pH 5·8–6.

Cultivation: deep digging, manure/compost at 1cwt per 10–12sq yd or in trenches.

Fertiliser: general at 2–3oz per sq yd broadcast or in drills.

Planting: plant tubers late February–late March in drills 5–6in deep, 12–15in apart, rows 2½ft apart, or in individual holes.

Cultivation in season: ridge up soil.

Harvest: lift tubers when required or when foliage dies down. Retain some tubers for next crop.

Pests: none of any consequence.

ARTICHOKES (Globe)

Permanent bed.

Lime: to pH 6·5.

Cultivation: single digging, manure at 1cwt per 10–12sq yd.

Fertiliser: general at 2–3oz per sq yd before planting.

Plant: detached offsets with good roots in mid-April 2½–3ft apart or sow seed in cold frames or greenhouse March–April or outdoors in May.

Cultivation in season: rotted manure/compost mulch in May and after planting. Allow no flowering first season. Hoe, but avoid drying out of beds. Remove dead leaves. In winter protect with peat/old compost.

Harvest: cut flower heads when ready.

Pests: none of any consequence.

BEANS, BROAD

Lime: to pH 6·5.

Sow: late October or March/April in drills 9–10in deep, drills 2½–3ft apart.

Seed: 1 pint per 100ft or 1cwt per acre.

Cultivation: deep digging. Manure at 1cwt per 10sq yd.

Fertiliser: general fertiliser with low nitrogen content at 3–4oz per sq yd. Use bonemeal (not general fertiliser) at 1oz per sq yd before autumn sowing.

Sow: hardy beans (mazagon or long pod) late October in mild areas. Protect with cloches in the North. Or March/April according to district and soil. Usually sown in rows 3ft apart × 6in apart.

Cultivation in season: regular hoeing and hand-weeding between plants. Pinch out growing points when plants are 3–4ft tall. Support in exposed areas with wide-mesh netting held by stakes or canes.

Harvest: June and through summer.

Pests, etc: black fly—nip growing points and use Malathion. Weevils (notches on leaves)—use BHC liquid or dust. 'Chocolate Spot' (blotches on leaves from April)—use Thiram preparations. Rust—use Dithane.

BEANS (HARICOT)

Need good weather, often impossible to grow in Scotland.

Seed: 1 pint per 100ft of single row (60lb per acre).

Cultivation: as for French beans but allow pods to hang till brown. Remove whole plant and hang upside down in shade or airy room to dry. Thrash seed or shake out of brittle pods. Store for winter use.

Pests, etc: see broad beans. Virus disease—use good seed to prevent.

CABBAGE

More of a field than market-garden crop for marketing. It is important to choose the correct variety for the time of year concerned.

Lime: to pH 6·5–6·8.

Seed: ¼–1oz per 100 plants, ½–¾lb for seed bed for transplanting, 4lb per acre for direct drilling (will vary according to variety spacing).

Cultivation: good well-prepared ground, applying farmyard manure as available.

Fertiliser: 3–4oz per sq yd, 6–8cwt per acre.

Spring Cabbage: sow in seed bed in July, plant 12in apart Sept/Oct. Cut May/June.

Early Summer Cabbage: sow in frame or greenhouse February/March, plant 18–24in apart in mid-April.

Autumn/Winter Cabbage: sow mid-late April out of doors, plant May/June 18–24in apart.

Cultivation in season: ridge ground to improve drainage of heavy land.

Pests, etc: cabbage caterpillar—BHC. Root fly—BHC. Green fly—Malathion, etc.

Target yield: 12,000 per acre (approx).

Value per acre: 12,000 @ 3p = £360.

CHIVES

Permanent bed. Grow almost anywhere. Split clumps and plant any time.

ENDIVES

Seed: for transplanting—$\frac{1}{5}$–$\frac{1}{4}$oz produces 50ft row of plants. Direct sowing 1oz per 100ft row (4lb per acre).
Cultivation: as for lettuce except for the early mid-August sowing when seedlings are planted in cold frame or under cloche 8–9in apart each way. Blanch hearts by inverting plate over plant till leaves are white.

HORSE RADISH

Cultivation: dig ground.
Lime: to pH 5.8–6.
Fertiliser: general at 2oz per sq yd in planting area.
Plant: March in holes made with long dibber, 1ft apart, deep enough to allow plants 4in soil covering.
Cultivation in season: hoeing.
Harvest: November. Store in sand or dry soil. Keep some for planting.

KALE (Borecole)

Seed: $\frac{1}{5}$–$\frac{1}{4}$oz produces 100 plants (see cabbage).
Cultivation: as for cabbage.
Fertiliser: as for cabbage.
Sowing: late April–mid-May in drills $\frac{1}{2}$in deep, 9–10in apart.
Plant: late June–late July 2$\frac{1}{2}$ft apart.
Cultivation in season: water, hoe.
Harvest: when leaves are large enough.
Pests, etc: see cabbage.

MINT

Special bed. Plant roots in March by spreading over surface. Cover with riddled soil $\frac{1}{2}$–$\frac{3}{4}$in deep. For winter supply lift

some roots, October/November and place in fish box and cover with 1in of soil. Place in warm greenhouse and water.
Pests, etc: mint rust—start with new stock.

PARSNIP

Seed: ½oz per 100ft row (3lb per acre).
Lime: to pH 6–6.3.
Cultivation: really deep digging, no manure (causes root forking). On poor land, narrow holes 12–15in deep (with crowbar). Fill with John Innes potting compost or mixture of sandy soil and fertiliser.
Fertiliser: general at 4–5oz per sq yd around sowing rows.
Sowing: February/early March in drills 1in deep, rows 12–15in apart. Where holes have been filled with compost sow 2–3 seeds.
Cultivation in season: thin or single out seedlings when large enough to handle to 3–4in apart. Hoe regularly and feed with fertiliser till growth is well advanced.
Harvest: delay until autumn frost (said to flavour roots).
Pests, etc: seldom, except rust (no cure).
Target yield: 9 tons per acre or 720 × 28lb.
Value per acre: 720 @ 50p = £360.

PEAS

Mostly grown on field scale.
Lime: to pH 6.5.
Sow: from February until mid-April in drills 2in deep, and 2–3ft apart (or further for stated varieties). Early crops can be grown under cloches.
Seed: 1 pint per 50–60ft row, 80–120lb per acre.
Cultivation: deep digging. Trench as for broad beans with rotted manure/compost 8–9in below the sowing area or apply manure/compost to land at 1cwt per 12–15sq yd.

Fertiliser: low nitrogen content, 2oz per sq yd (4–5cwt per acre) or strips 1ft wide in vicinity of sowing drill. No fertiliser inside drill.

Cultivation in season: hoeing, hand-weeding, watering, supports if necessary (twigs or wire-mesh netting). Mulch with grass cuttings (if not treated with hormone weedkiller).

Pests, etc: mildew—use Karathane. Pea midge, pea moth, pea and bean weevil—use BHC dust.

Target yield: $2\frac{1}{2}$–3 tons per acre.

Value per acre: 5,600lb @ 4p = £224.

POTATOES

Early crops can be quite lucrative, being planted from February until March.

Lime: to pH 5·6 in well-manured land.

Seed: early varieties—1 stone per 80ft. Mid and late varieties —1 stone per 100ft. $\frac{3}{4}$–1 ton per acre.

Cultivation: deep digging advantageous. Otherwise dig land to one spit without manure, saving this for scattering in trenches.

Fertiliser: apply potato fertiliser in or adjacent to drills at 3–4oz per yd of drill (8–9cwt per acre) then rake in.

Plant: early—March/April. Main-crop—from April. Avoid frost. Use spade or draw hoe or ridger to make V-shaped trench 5–6in deep. Early potatoes—1ft apart, rows 19–21in apart. Main-crop—15in apart, rows 26–30in apart. Place tubers in trench with shoots, if any, uppermost. Sprout early potatoes in light frost-proof place. At planting time remove all but two shoots. Cut large potatoes lengthwise so that each section has at least two sprouts. Smear cut surface with flowers of sulphur to avoid fungal infection. Close drills with rake or spade.

Cultivation in season: earth up with draw hoe when shoots

appear, using paraquat weedkiller. Continue through season until drills are earthed up 10–12in.

Harvest: lift early potatoes when tubers are large enough, later varieties September/October. For storing, lift and dry potatoes, store in sacks or pits in the open. Keep sacked potatoes frost-free.

Pests, etc: potato blight—use Bordeaux mixture or Dithane in June (south) or July (north). Wart disease—grow immune varieties. Black leg (turns stems mushy)—spray early with Bordeaux mixture. Eelworm—control by crop rotation. Wireworms (bore into tubers)—BHC. Slugs—slug pellets.

Target yield: 10 tons per acre.

Value per acre: 10 tons @ £15 = £150.

SHALLOTS

Seed: 2–3lb per 50ft row.

Cultivation: rich, well-consolidated soil (see onions).

Lime: to pH 5·8–6.

Fertiliser: general at 4–5oz per sq yd or applied in strips.

Plant: February/March. Push bulbs into land 6–8in apart, rows 12in apart.

Cultivation in season: hoeing.

Harvest: July/August. When leaves yellow, insert fork under bulbs to sever roots. Dry bulbs like onions ripe. Split up and plait for storage.

Pests, etc: see onions.

SPINACH

Not a highly lucrative crop. Two types—summer and winter varieties. Excellent inter-crop between pea or celery rows.

Seed: 1oz per 50–60ft row (20–30lb per acre).

Lime: to pH 6·5–6·8.

Cultivation: digging, manure/compost at 1cwt per 10sq yd.

Fertiliser: general at 3–4oz per sq yd before sowing.

Sowing: First sowing of early summer type (south) early March, (north) mid-March. Repeat every 3–4 weeks until July—then winter types. Sow in drills 1in deep, 12–18in apart. Thin seedlings to 6–8in apart.

Cultivation in season: hoeing, nitro-chalk at 1oz per 10ft row after thinning.

Harvest: when leaves are large but not coarse.

Pests, etc: mildew—use Dithane. Leaf-tunnelling marigold fly—use DDT at first sign. Sucking aphids—use Malathion.

SUGAR CORN

Grown for seed heads. Enjoys a limited demand, but can be lucrative.

Cultivation: good, well-drained land.

Lime: to pH 6·5–6·8.

Fertiliser: general at 3–4oz per sq yd before sowing or planting.

Sowing: in small composition pots mid-April. Germinate in cold frame in the south or in slightly heated greenhouse in the north.

Plant: late May to mid-June. Planting distance out of doors 18in × 3ft. Sowing direct is also practised, sowing two seeds at each station.

Seed requirement: ¼lb per 100ft row. 12lb per acre.

Cultivation in season: grow in lee of high-growing crop. Water and protect from wind. When cobs form, shake pollen from male flowers on to tassels protruding from female cobs. Liquid feed.

Harvest: when ripe.

Pests, etc: none of any consequence.

VEGETABLE MARROW

(Also Courgettes.)
Special beds.
Seed: bought by number.
Lime: to pH 6.
Cultivation: holes 2ft wide, 8–9in deep, 3–4ft apart filled with compost or rotted manure.
Fertiliser: unnecessary if holes are filled with compost or manure. Apply feeding when growth begins.
Sowing: early April in gentle heat in individual pots. Place seed sideways.
Plant: harden off and set in middle of the heap of compost/manure, slightly above ground level, end May/early June. Moisture then runs off rather than rots stem. Plant 4ft apart. Cloches assist early establishment. Frequent liquid feeding once growth begins.
Cultivation in season: detach male blooms (those without small marrow) and dust pollen on to female blooms. Take only 3–4 marrows per plant.
Harvest: if necessary turn to sun to ripen.
Pests, etc: red spider—use good general insecticide (see cucumber).

VEGETABLE PLANTS FOR SALE

There can be a good demand for vegetable plants—brassicas, leeks, onions, celery and to a lesser extent lettuce—for sale at the planting stage. For costs of production refer to the preceding notes on seed costs, etc.

'FORCED' VEGETABLES

Many vegetables can be forced in sheds or under greenhouse benches in darkness, including the following:

Seakale
Plants are lifted in the autumn, and after removal of side-shoots the main plants are covered to a depth of 3in with good soil or old manure, and given heat and darkness.

Asparagus
Asparagus can also be lifted in and placed under a 3in layer of peat.

Mint
Mint too can be forced in boxes.

Rhubarb (forced)
This is a major crop and so is now dealt with in more detail.

Culture: lift crowns in October/early November and place on soil surface to become frosted. (A 'points' system is used.) In late November/December/January pack crowns in a completely dark place with plenty of water at a temperature of 50°F (10°C). Three-year-old crowns are grown in field for forcing.

Target yield: 2 tons per 1,000sq ft in forcing shed.

Packaging: lettuce crates, 1½ stone per crate.

Crop costs and returns per 1,000sq ft in forcing shed

Revenue—320 stone @ £1.05	£336	
Less commission @ 10%	34	
Less crop expenses:		£302
Crowns—1,500 @ £5/100		75
*Fertiliser—2cwt sulphate of ammonia @ £1.5		3
8cwt compound @ £2.6		21
Sprays—as required		6
Packaging—214 @ 8.5p		18
Carriage—214 @ 5p		11
*For outdoor period.		£134

Page 117 (above) This diminutive greenhouse, equipped with electric tubular heaters, is in use for twelve months of the year for propagation and pot plant culture; (below) Dutch light greenhouses are cheap and efficient, as also are Dutch light sashes for making cold frames. Here is Ian G. Walls' unit at Milngavie which has produced countless crops of tomatoes, lettuce and other crops over the last fifteen years.

Page 118 (*above*) One way of overcoming high heating costs on a small scale is to use a separately heated propagator. Here is the Humex 'Big Top' unit; (*below*) frames have an important role to play in both amateur gardening and commercial growing. Here is a frame unit equipped with both soil warming and air warming (Humex).

Margin per 1,000sq ft of glass: £168
Labour requirement per 1,000sq ft: 141 hours, heaviest months January (64 hours), February and December (28 hours each).
Margin per hour worked: £1.19

VEGETABLES UNDER GLASS

A constant demand, but competition from imports is increasing.

Cucumbers

Culture: seed sown from December onwards individually in $2\frac{1}{2}$in pots filled with compost. Can be sown in cold frames in late April. Transfer glasshouse crop to 5in pots at end of December and plant out in February 2ft apart in prepared beds, and in succession for later crops. Frame or cloche crops should be planted out in late May or early June. For outdoor crops sow in cold frame in late April/early May, using small pots. Harden off for setting out in mid-June, 3–4ft apart each way.

Cultivation in season: constant feeding with complete liquid feed. Train plants. If one plant per frame, allow shoot to grow to four corners, then pinch out growing-point to encourage side branching. If two per frame, train leading shoots to two corners and pinch out. Pruning will be necessary. Nip off male flowers (usually on main stem and without embryo cucumber at flower base) or grow all-female varieties. Tie greenhouse crop to wires led across greenhouse 9–10in apart, or train single stem on string (as for tomatoes) $2\frac{1}{2}$–3ft apart if on 'square' plant.

Pests, etc: for white fly and red spider use Malathion. 'Smoke bombs' are available for glasshouses. Mildew—use Karathane. To prevent rotting at neck of plant, plant with root ball proud of soil.

Temperatures: glasshouse crop—75–80°F (23·9–26·7°C) dur-

H

ing germination. Reduce to 65°F (18·3°C) minimum.

Preparation of beds: make up beds using the following per 1,000sq ft.

> 2 tons straw
> 2 tons farmyard manure
> ½cwt base fertiliser
> ½cwt lime

Plant on top of beds in rows 5ft apart, plants 2ft apart, giving 100 plants per 1,000sq ft.

Soil sterilisation: required annually.

Target yield: 5,000 cucumbers per 1,000sq ft.

Packaging: cardboard boxes lined with paper. Average fourteen cucumbers per box.

Successional crops: chrysanthemums, Christmas bulbs, pot plants (Christmas).

Cost and returns per 1,000sq ft (for glasshouse culture)

Revenue—5,000 @ 7p	£350	
Less commission @ 10%	35	
		£315
Less crop expenses:		
Seed—100 @ 5p		5
Pots (depreciation)		1
Compost		1
Soil sterilisation—estimated cost		5
Bed and fertiliser		14
Fuel—35sec—1,500gal @ 8p		120
Sprays, support, etc		3
Packaging—322 @ 5p		16
Carriage—322 @ 4p		13
		£178

Margin per 1,000sq ft: £137

Labour requirement: 342 hours, heaviest months April and May (45 hours each), June, July, August (40 hours each).

Margin per hour worked: £0.4

Cost of glasshouse and equipment: £800

No of years to repay capital cost: $\frac{800}{137} = 5.8$ years

Note: Cucumbers in cold frames frequently follow a crop of lettuce—and yields are commercially lower, the same being true of cloche-grown crops. Capital costs are of course much lower.

Tomatoes

Always enjoy an excellent demand, but competition from imports.

Culture: for main-crop production, seed should be sown late December in seed trays. Two weeks later seedlings should be pricked out and potted up into $3\frac{1}{2}$in (or $4\frac{1}{4}$in) pots. As the plants grow the pots should be spaced out to prevent leaves overlapping. When the first flower is showing (mid to late March) the crop is ready for planting. Picking should start about the middle of May and continue until about the end of October. For early crop sow in mid-November, plant February.

Temperature: 65°F (18.3°C) during germination, then drop to a minimum of 57°F (13.9°C) until planting, when it should be increased to 56–58°F (13–14°C) night, 66–67°F (19°C) day, ventilating at 72–74°F (22–23°C) until the end of the season.

Soil sterilisation: soil must be sterilised, either with steam using a steam boiler and grid pipes, or by chemicals.

Plant spacing: 300 plants per 1,000sq ft, 15in between plants. Rows 30in apart.

Fertiliser: base at $1\frac{1}{2}$cwt per 1,000sq ft.

Liquid—60lb potassium nitrate
15lb ammonium nitrate
or proprietary liquid feed at
recommended rates. Dry
feeding can also be used.
} 1 in 200 in water per 1,000 sq ft

Support and training: the tomato plants are supported by strings attached to wires in the roof of the glasshouse. Each week the plant should be twisted round the string and all side-shoots removed. Layering systems are now widely practiced.

Target yield: 24cwt per 1,000sq ft—220 boxes × 12lb.

Packaging: cardboard boxes lined with paper, and with covers, 12lb per box.

Costs and returns per 1,000sq ft

Revenue—220 boxes @ £1.25	£275	
(9lb per plant)		
Less commission @ 10%	28	
Less crop expenses:	——	£247
Seed—$\frac{1}{10}$oz @ £15		2
Compost		1
Pots—3½in—300 @ £3/1,000		1
Soil sterilisation, estimated cost		10
Fertiliser—base		1
Liquid*		3
Peat—10cwt @ 35p		4
Fuel oil, 35sec.—1,300 @ 8p		104
Twine, sprays, water, etc		4
Packaging—220 @ 5p		11
Carriage—220 @ 4p		9
		£150

Margin per 1,000sq ft: £97

Labour requirement: 131 hours, heaviest months June (24 hours), July (18 hours).

Margin per hour worked: £0.74

Cost of glasshouse and equipment: £800

No of years to repay capital cost: $\frac{800}{97}$ = 8 years

*Proprietary feeds at cost.

Note: Later crops of tomatoes can of course be grown with various levels of heat, planting cold in April/May, and while yields are generally lower (5–7lb per plant) there is no heating bill for the growing stage (this excludes cost of plant raising). Double-cropping can also be carried out, removing an early crop in June and planting tomatoes again. Growing systems involving peat troughs are now popular and will affect the economic picture, the cost of setting up the system being offset by avoidance of sterilisation costs.

Peppers (green or red—capsicums)

These are an increasingly popular vegetable to grow under glass. Culture and economics are broadly similar to tomatoes. They are also an ideal crop for plastic structures.

Cultural programme: date sown—mid-March; Planting—mid-May; Cropping—August-October.

Seed: sown direct into 3½in pots using John Innes Potting No 2.

Temperature: minimum night temperature of 50°F (10°C) until planting. Thereafter no heating required.

Support: twine and wires.

Spacing: 14,500 plants per acre or 330 per 1,000sq ft.

Fertiliser: as for tomatoes.

Yield: 4·4lb per plant or 28 tons per acre or 120 12lb boxes per 1,000sq ft.

Costs and returns per 1,000sq ft

Revenue—120 boxes @ £1.30	£156	
Less crop expenses:	——	£156
Seed—⅓oz @ £8	0.5	
Pots—(3 year depreciation)		
330 @ £7/1,000	0.8	
Compost—0·2cu yd @ £5	1.0	
Fuel oil—120gal 950sec. oil @ 5p	6.0	
Fuel for sterilising—30gal @ 5p	1.5	

Farmyard manure—7 tons @ £2	14.0	
Fertiliser base	1.5	
Fertiliser liquid	2.0	
Twine and wires	2.0	
Water, estimated	0.5	
Electricity @ 10% of fuel oil cost	0.8	
Packaging—120 tomato boxes @ 5p	6.0	
Carriage—120 boxes @ 4p	4.8	£ 41
Gross margin		£115

Labour requirement: similar to tomatoes.

Lettuce (winter and spring)

Culture: successional crops of lettuce can be grown over the winter, starting with an autumn-sown crop cut for the Christmas market, and carrying on until the late spring, just before the first of the early outdoor crops come to market. Seed is sown in boxes using seed compost, and three weeks later are transplanted into the glasshouse at a spacing of 8 x 8in, giving approximately 2,000 plants per 1,000sq ft, allowing for paths. Typical dates for sowing and planting are given below: (Christmas crops only for good light areas in modern structures). Timing will vary according to region.

	Winter crop	*Early spring crop*	*Late spring crop*
Sown	1 September	1 January	20 March
Planted	21 September	21 January	10 April
Harvested	Mid-December	Mid-March	Late May
Temperatures:	Minimum of 45°F (7·2°C)	Minimum of 40°F (4·4°C)	No heat

Production per 1,000sq ft

Total number of lettuce	2,000	2,000	2,000
Less wastage	20% 400	10% 200	5% 100
Total production	1,600	1,800	1,900

Packaging:

Winter crop	Early spring crop	Late spring crop
cardboard boxes	cardboard boxes	lettuce crates
12 per box	12 per box	average 20 per crate
individually in	individually in	—
polythene bags	polythene bags	

Costs and returns per 1,000sq ft

	Total	Winter		Early Spring		Late Spring	
Revenue							
(5,300 lettuce)	£218	1,600 @ 5p	£80	1,800 @ 4p	£72	1,900 @ 3½p	£66
Less commission							
@ 10%	22		8		7		7
	£196		£72		£65		£59

Less crop expenses:

	Total	Winter		Early Spring		Late Spring	
Seed ½oz @ £3	3		1		1		1
Fertiliser 42lb							
@ 4p	2		1		1		—
Fuel oil 35sec.	35	260 @ 8p	21	180 @ 8p	14		—
Compost, sprays	6		2		2		2
Packaging	23	134 @ 5p	7	150 @ 5p	8	95 crates @ 8½p	8
3,910 bags							
@ £4/1,000	14		7		7		—
Carriage	19		6		7		6
	£102		£45		£40		£17
Margin per							
1,000sq ft	£94		£27		£25		£42

Labour requirement: *Winter*, 34 hours, heaviest months September (14 hours), December (13 hours); *early spring*, 30 hours (14 hours each January and March, 2 hours February); *late spring*, 26 hours (11 hours April, 10 hours May, 5 hours March).

Margin per hour worked: £1.04

Lettuce can be grown on a continuous basis under glass or plastic structures, especially with the use of a growing room for the propagation period, so that plants can be quickly raised to replace the harvested crops. Pelleted seed, in soil or peat blocks, makes for labour saving.

Fruit Crops

Out of Doors

The situation of a garden is a key factor in profitable fruit growing, especially for strawberries. A sheltered area producing early crops allows them to be sold at near-monopoly prices. The use of polythene tunnels can bring forward the production period for strawberries by 2–3 weeks or more. Conversely shading to give 'short days' can delay cropping (see page 132).

Climate is also an important factor. Orchard fruits are not worthwhile in Scotland or the north of England, except on a small scale for domestic use, with the possible exception of plums. Soft fruits, however, can be grown successfully almost anywhere in the country, although the drier areas in the east are best.

One disadvantage with fruit, although it can apply to other crops as well, is the constant work necessary during the very short marketing season, and finding labour can be a problem. There is an increasing market for freshly picked fruit for deep freezing, and self-picking schemes are becoming popular.

APPLES (cooking)

Culture: apples can be grown as standards, half-standards or, for easier management, in dwarf pyramid or 'spindle' forms. Good initial cultivation of the soil, plus careful preparation and planting, regular manuring, pruning and spraying, with grassing-down after a few years, is the general routine. Weed control is a specialised matter. The culture of apples, and indeed many other fruits, is a specialised subject and readers are advised to seek further information.

Spacing: 15 × 15ft or 190 per acre (dwarf pyramids 4–5ft apart in rows 6–8ft apart).

Establishment period: 6–8 years.

Life of crop: indefinite.

Sprays: as required.

Target yield: 300 bushels per acre.

Packaging: bushel boxes (40lb each).

Crop costs and returns per acre

Revenue—300 @ £1	£300	
Less commission @ 10%	£30	
Less crop expenses:		£270
Fertiliser—8cwt general @ £2.5		20
Sprays—as required		8
Packaging—300 boxes @ 15p		45
Carriage—300 boxes @ 10p		30
		£103

Margin per acre: £167

Labour requirement: 240 hours, heaviest months December (110 hours), September (40 hours).

Margin per hour worked: £0.70

APPLES (dessert)

Culture: as for cooking apples.

Target yield: 300 bushels per acre.

Packaging: ½ bushel boxes (20lb each).

Crop costs and returns per acre (established orchard)

Revenue—300 @ £1.8	£540	
Less commission @ 10%	54	
		£486
Less crop expenses:		
Fertiliser—8cwt general @ £2.5	20	
Sprays—as required	8	
Packaging—600 @ 10p	60	
Carriage—600 @ 5p	30	
		£118

Margin per acre: £368

Labour requirement: 315 hours, heaviest months December (95 hours), October (50 hours).

Margin per hour worked: £1.20

BLACKCURRANTS (for processing)

Culture: blackcurrants (obtained as certified stock) are planted from October until February in well-manured ground at 5 × 5ft (1,743 per acre). Prune back branches after planting and cut out old wood each autumn after fruiting.

An annual dressing of 4–5oz per sq yd (10cwt per acre) of general fertiliser is given in March. They can be a very lucrative crop but tend to be subject to seasonal variation in both demand and price.

Target yield: 2 tons per acre.

Crop costs and returns per acre

Revenue—2 tons @ £140		£280
Less crop expenses:		
Bushes over 10 years, 1,743 @ £25/1,000	4	
Fertiliser—10cwt compound @ £2.8	28	
Sprays—as required	25	
		£57

Margin per acre: £223

Labour requirement: 320 hours, heaviest months August (115 hours), July (80 hours).

Margin per hour worked: £0.70

GOOSEBERRIES

Culture: plant from October until February in well-manured ground at 5 × 5ft (1,743 per acre). Prune in February by spurring and top dress with 3oz per sq yd of general fertiliser. This crop is subject to extremely varied demand.

Target yield: $3\frac{1}{2}$ tons per acre—650 × 12lb.

Packaging: cardboard boxes—12lb per box.

Crop costs and returns per acre (established plantation)

Revenue—650 boxes @ 60p	£390	
Less commission @ 10%	39	
		£351
Less crop expenses:		
Cost of bushes over 10 years, 1,743 @ £25/1,000		4
Fertiliser—6cwt @ £3		18
Sprays—as required		10
Packaging—650 @ 5p		33
Carriage—650 @ 4p		26
		£91

Margin per acre: £260

Labour requirement: 375 hours, heaviest months August (85 hours), July (80 hours).

Margin per hour worked: £0.70

PEARS

Culture and economics are very similar to dessert apples (page 127), the most popular style of bush being a dwarf pyramid or spindle, planted 4–5ft apart in rows 6–8ft apart.

Pears are also frequently grown in gardens as half-standard or standard bushes; where they are allowed to look after themselves, they may yield very spasmodically.

PLUMS

Culture: the culture of plums is basically similar to apples, regarding good land, weed-control measures and eventual grassing-down. Spacing for half-standard trees is 18 × 18ft (134 per acre).

Target yield: 800 × 12lb per acre.

Packaging: cardboard boxes, 12lb per box.

Establishment cost: 134 trees/acre = £60
+ Fertiliser = £30

Crop costs and returns per acre (established orchard)

Revenue—9,600lb @ 5p	£480	
Less commission @ 10%	48	
Less crop expenses:		£432
Cost of trees (over 10 years)		10
Fertiliser—8cwt general @ £2.5		20
Sprays—as required		8
Packaging—800 boxes @ 5p		40
Carriage—800 boxes @ 4p		32
		£110

Margin per acre: £322

Labour requirement: 180 hours, heaviest months August (55 hours), September (50 hours).

Margin per hour worked: £1.80

RASPBERRIES

Culture: 3,600 canes per acre. Raspberries are a crop which thrive in most areas, but particularly in the cooler drier areas; in the east of Scotland, for instance, raspberries grown to perfection are a major crop. Soil should be well prepared and in good order before planting certified stock in either autumn or spring. Routine culture consists of pruning in the autumn, tying in, mulching with farmyard manure and moulding the soil over it, the application of Simazine weedkiller and applications of paraquat where necessary on an inter-row basis.

Life of plantation: 8 years.

Target yield: 2 tons per acre (8 year average).

Packaging: 2lb chips.

Crop costs and returns per acre

Revenue—4,480lb @ 12½p*	£560	
Less commission @ 10%	56	
Less crop expenses:		£504
Canes (over 8 years) 3,600 @ £1.6/1,000	7	
Posts and wire (over 8 years)	5	
Fertiliser—4cwt compound @ £2.8	11	
Weedkiller—½lb Simazine @ £1.5lb	1	
2 pints paraquat @ £1/pint	2	
Sprays—as required	4	
Packaging—2,240 @ 3p	67	
Carriage—2,240 @ 2p	45	
		£142

Margin per acre: £362

Labour requirement: 992 hours, heaviest months July (420 hours), August (400 hours).

Margin per hour worked: £0.36

*Very much higher returns possible on retail selling.

STRAWBERRIES

Culture: strawberries are planted in autumn or spring, the usual spacing being 3ft × 14in or 30 × 18in to give approximately 12,000 plants per acre. On a large scale they are machine-planted. Light dressings of 4cwt per acre of compound fertiliser are applied in March/April and weedkiller applied in either autumn or spring (see appendix). The main scourge with strawberries is botrytis or fruit rot, necessitating regular spraying with Benlate or Elvaron.

Life of crop: 4 years.

Target yield: 45cwt (average over 4 years).

Packaging: 2lb chips.

Crop costs and returns per acre

Revenue—5,600lb @ 15p	£840	
Less commission @ 10%	84	
		£756
Less crop expenses:		
Runners (over 4 years) 12,000 @ £4/1,000	12	
Fertiliser—4cwt compound @ £2.8	11	
Sprays—as required	8	
Packaging—2,800 @ 3p	84	
Carriage—2,800 @ 2p	56	
	£171	

Margin per acre: £585

Labour requirement: 986 hours, heaviest months July (457 hours), June (198 hours).

Margin per hour worked: £0.59

Early strawberry growing under polythene tunnels is now becoming popular. While yields can be lower, prices received are generally high, due to earliness. Strawberries can also be grown under glass, being planted at 10 × 10in in September. Shading with black polythene to give 'short days' can delay flowering and fruiting.

Other Fruit Crops

Other outdoor fruit crops grown include loganberries and red currants, for both of which there is a limited demand.

Under Glass

Peaches, nectarines, strawberries, vines and melons are frequently grown in greenhouses for home use, wine-making and limited sale. They are not considered as commercially viable crops in the UK, however, as they can be produced very much cheaper in favourable climates out of doors. In these warmer climates their culture tends to be a highly specialised business and cultural details relative to the district in which they are grown must be followed.

STRAWBERRIES UNDER GLASS

A specialised crop in some areas.

Culture: maiden runners (deblossomed one-year-old plants), or alternatively cold-stored runners, are planted up in September in the greenhouse border, 12 x 12in apart in 4-row-wide beds, polythene-covered, with 2ft 6in path, in well-prepared soil. They are watered in and kept as cool as possible until January when the temperature in the greenhouse is gradually raised to about 50°F (10°C) night and 60°F (15·6°C) day. Regular watering is essential, along with full ventilation, to encourage pollination during the flowering period.

Target yield: 2 tons per acre = 17,920 punnets x ¼lb.

Packaging: ¼lb punnets in 3lb cardboard trays.

Costs and returns per acre

Revenue—17,920 punnets @ 15p	£2,688	
Less commission @ 10%	268	
Less crop expenses:		£2,420
Runners—13,000 @ £10/1,000		130
Fertiliser and sprays		120
Water		24
Polythene sheeting		90
Fuel heating—9,000gal @ 5p		450
Electricity—heating		45
Packaging—punnets 124 gross @ 55p/gross		68
trays 1,500 @ 5p		75
Carriage—1,500 @ 6p		90
		£1,092

Margin per acre: £1,328

Labour requirement: 977 hours, heaviest months April (450 hours), May (190 hours).

Margin per hour worked: £1.36

Note: Plastic structures and mobile greenhouses are being increasingly used.

Page 135 (above) Pot chrysanthemums are not for the 'amateur' and must be considered on a professional basis if quality is to be high enough to enjoy a ready sale in competition with pot chrysanthemums from specialist producers. The angle steel bench and expanded metal top is of interest in this direction; (below) shrub growing can be extremely profitable, especially in favourable areas. Here is part of the Highlands & Islands Development Board experimental unit at Sir William Lithgow's Ormsary Estate in Argyllshire, where the weather, although windy, is extremely mild and frost incidence low.

Page 136 (above) Soil-warmed frames can produce early crops of lettuce in quantity. Here is a unit in a garden at Edinburgh; *(below)* cacti enjoy an increasing demand and are available in a wide range of types and varieties. Here is a small unit almost entirely devoted to the culture of cacti at Eaglesham, Renfrewshire.

Bulbs for Forcing

DAFFODILS, TULIPS

Culture: bulbs, pre-cooled for Christmas or uncooled for spring sale, are tightly planted in boxes filled with fresh soil or compost in October, the box is then covered with ½–1in of sand, placed outside and covered with soil (previously mixed with peat and sand) to a depth of 6in (straw is sometimes used). Pre-cooled bulbs are brought into the glasshouse the third week in November for Christmas flowering. Thereafter uncooled bulbs should be brought in in batches at fortnightly intervals to give a succession of flowers for sale throughout the spring.

Temperature: minimum heat to prevent frost until flower bud can be felt in shoot, then increase to 65°F (18·3°C) gradually.

Production from 1,000sq ft: (a) daffodils—3 batches × 1 ton, yielding 20,000 blooms/ton; (b) tulips—3 batches × 20,000 bulbs, yielding 18,000 blooms/batch.

Packaging: cardboard flower boxes in bunches of 5 blooms, 20 bunches per box, lined with paper.

Period occupied: November until April.

Possible successional crops: tomatoes, cucumbers (in pots), pot plants.

Costs and returns per 1,000sq ft: *Daffodils*

	Total	Pre-cooled	2 batches uncooled
Revenue	12,000 bunches	4,000 bunches	8,000 bunches
	£1,320	@ 15p £600	@ 9p £720

	Total	Pre-cooled		2 batches uncooled	
Less commission					
@ 10%	132		60		72
	£1,188		£540		£648
Less crop expenses:					
Bulbs 3 tons @ £210	630	1 ton @ £250	250	2 tons @ £190	380
Fuel 1,000gal @ 8p	80		27		53
Boxes 1,200 @ 3p					
(2 years)	18		6		12
Compost 7cu yd					
@ £5.5	39		13		26
Peat & sand as reqd.	9		3		6
Packaging 600 @ 7.5p	45	200 @ 7.5p	15	400 @ 7.5p	30
Carriage 600 @ 5p	30	200 @ 5p	10	400 @ 5p	20
	£851		£324		£527
Margin per					
1,000sq ft	£337		£216		£121

Labour requirement: *pre-cooled*, 235 hours (heaviest month December, 150 hours); *uncooled* (1st batch), 235 hours (heaviest months February, March, 75 hours); *uncooled* (2nd batch), 235 hours, heaviest month April (150 hours).

Margin per hour worked: £0.48

Estimated cost of lean-to glasshouse and equipment: £700

No of years to repay above cost $\frac{700}{337} = 2 \cdot 1$ years.

Costs and returns per 1,000sq ft: *Tulips*

	Total	Pre-cooled		2 batches uncooled	
Revenue	10,800 bunches	3,600 bunches		7,200 bunches	
	£1,872	@ 20p £720		@ 16p £1,152	
Less commission					
@ 10%	187		72		115
	£1,685		£648		£1,037
Less crop expenses:					
Bulbs 60,000		20,000 @		40,000 @	
	1,080	£20/1,000	400	£17/1,000	680
Fuel 1,000gal @ 8p	80		27		53

	Total	Pre-cooled	2 batches uncooled
Boxes 1,200			
@ 3p (2yrs)	18	6	12
Compost 7cu yd			
@ £5.5	39	13	26
Peat & sand as reqd.	9	3	6
Packaging 540 @ 7.6p	41	180 @ 7.6p 14	360 @ 7.6p 27
Carriage 540 @ 5p	27	180 @ 5p 9	360 @ 5p 18
	£1,294	£472	£822
Margin per			
1,000sq ft	£391	£176	£215

Labour requirement: *pre-cooled*, 220 hours (heaviest month December, 145 hours); *uncooled* (1st batch), 220 hours (heaviest month March, 73 hours); *uncooled* (2nd batch), 220 hours (heaviest month April, 145 hours).

Margin per hour worked: £0.62

Estimated cost of lean-to glasshouse and equipment (1,000 sq ft)—£700.

Number of years to repay above cost $\frac{700}{391} = 1 \cdot 8$ years.

TULIPS—5° direct planted

Culture: specially treated (5°) bulbs must be obtained. These are planted direct into the glasshouse in early November. Soil temperature at time of planting should be around 50°F (10°C) rising to 60°F (15·6°C) by the beginning of December. Air temperature should be low at time of planting but gradually raised to 70°F (21·1°C) by the beginning of December.

Target yield: 12,000 bulbs per 1,000sq ft are planted.

Less wastage $7\frac{1}{2}\% = 11,100$ blooms or 2,220 bunches.

Packaging: bunches of 5—average 20 bunches per cardboard box, lined with paper.

Crop costs and returns

Revenue—2,220 bunches @ 25p	£555	
Less commission @ 10%	55	
		£500
Less crop expenses:		
Bulbs—12,000 bulbs @ £27/1,000		324
Fuel—400gal @ 7p		28
Sprays—as required		4
Packaging—111 boxes @ 8p		9
Carriage—111 boxes @ 5p		6
		£371

Margin per 1,000sq ft: £129

Labour requirement: 95 hours, heaviest month December (80 hours).

Margin per hour worked: £1.37

HYACINTHS (for the Christmas market)

Culture: 16–17cm bulbs prepared for early flowering are boxed in late September/early October in well-textured compost with a pH of over 6. Bulbs are covered under the compost almost touching (approximately 18 bulbs per standard seed tray). Boxes are then well watered, planted out in beds, and covered first of all with a layer of sand (to form barrier) and then 6in of sand/peat with a pH of 6·2–6·5 and in addition a layer of straw. Water may be required in dry warm weather to reduce temperature. After 6 weeks (3rd week November) bulbs are lifted into the greenhouse at 50°F (10°C) and kept shaded to extend flower spikes. The temperature is raised gradually to 65–70°F (18·3–21·1°C) and maintained there for 9–11 days, when the temperature is then lowered. Bulbs are watered carefully, taking care to avoid watering into the neck of the bulbs. They are then planted in 6in bowls with ferns or other plants for marketing over the Christmas period. Bulbs can also be grown in individual peat pots.

Production from 1,000sq ft: 2,000 bowls × 4 bulbs

Less wastage 5%   100

    Target yield   1,900 bowls

Packaging: cardboard boxes, 6 bowls per box.

Costs and returns per 1,000sq ft

Revenue—1,900 bowls @ 65p	£1,235	
Less commission @ 10%	124	
		£1,111
Less crop expenses:		
Bulbs (4 per bowl) 8,000 @ £80/1,000		640
Fern—2,000 @ 4p		80
Bowl—1,900 @ 6p		114
Compost—10cwt @ 90p		9
Boxes—depreciation		8
Fuel oil—300gal @ 8p		24
Packaging—317 @ 12½p		40
Carriage—317 @ 5p		16
		£931

Margin per 1,000sq ft: £180

Labour requirement: 155 hours, heaviest month December (100 hours).

Margin per hour worked: £1.16

OTHER BULB CROPS

Other bulb crops grown under glass include: early gladioli, iris, arum lilies, clivias, chincherinchees, lily of the valley (for forcing), snowdrops, ixias, liliums, montbretia, muscari, nerines, ranunculus, schizostylis (kaffir lily), sparaxis.

Their culture requires attention to detail and the economics of growing them revolve almost entirely around securing a specialist outlet.

Chrysanthemums

Culture: Chrysanthemums for autumn and Christmas flowering can be planted either direct into the glasshouse from July on, or can be started off in frames and transplanted into the glasshouse at a later date. They can be grown either as:

    (a) single-stem—planted mid-August

    (b) 2-stem—planted end July

    (c) 3-stem at most—planted mid-July

Two or more stems are obtained by removing the 'break' bud two weeks after planting and allowing the required number of side-stems to develop. Thereafter for 'standards' all other buds are removed to prevent further side-shoots developing. Another alternative is to allow six top stems to develop, this being sold as a 'spray' rather than single blooms (involving spray varieties).

Temperature: 56°F (13·3°C) minimum for six weeks and thereafter 50°F (10°C).

Fertiliser: 4oz per sq yd of general fertiliser before planting. One liquid feed during the growing period.

Sprays: against red spider, etc—use an insecticide containing Demeton-S-Methyl.

Support: nylon netting.

Production from 1,000 sq ft:

    (a) single-stem, 5 x 5in, 4,500 plants yielding 4,000 blooms

    (b) 2-stem, 7 x 8in, 1,900 plants yielding 3,000 blooms

    (c) 3-stem, 9 x 9in, 1,300 plants yielding 3,000 blooms

    (d) sprays, 5 x 5in, 4,500 plants yielding 4,000 sprays

Packaging: cardboard flower boxes lined with paper, 6

blooms per bunch, average 5 per box. Sprays average 24 per box.

Costs and returns per 1,000sq ft: single-stem crops

Revenue—667 bunches @ 35p	£233	
Less commission @ 10%	23	
		£210
Less crop expenses:		
Cuttings—4,500 @ £20/1,000		90
Fertiliser—¼cwt @ £2.8 + Liquid feed		1
Sprays—as required		1
Netting—100sq yd (over 7 years)		1
Fuel—35 second—250 @ 8p		20
Packaging—127 @ 10p		13
Carriage—127 @ 5p		6
		£132

Margin per 1,000sq ft: £78

Labour requirement: 60 hours, heaviest month December (20 hours).

Margin per hour worked: £1.30

Costs and returns per 1,000sq ft: 2-stem crops

Revenue—500 bunches @ 35p	£175	
Less commission @ 10%	18	
		£157
Less crop expenses:		
Cuttings—1,900 @ £20/1,000		38
Fertiliser (as for single-stem crop)		1
Sprays—as required		1
Netting (as for single-stem crop)		1
Fuel (as for single-stem crop)		20
Packaging—100 @ 10p		10
Carriage—100 @ 5p		5
		£76

Margin per 1,000sq ft: £81

Labour requirement: 70 hours, heaviest month December

(20 hours). Add 30 hours for transplanting if started in frames.

Margin per hour worked: £1.16

Costs and returns per 1,000sq ft: 3-stem crops

Revenue—500 bunches @ 30p	£150	
Less commission @ 10%	15	
		£135
Less crop expenses:		
Cuttings—1,300 @ £20/1,000		26
Fertiliser (as 1-stem crop)		1
Sprays—as required		1
Netting (as for 1-stem crop)		1
Fuel (as for 1-stem crop)		20
Packaging—134 @ 10p		10
Carriage—134 @ 5p		5
		£64

Margin per 1,000sq ft: £71

Labour requirement: 70 hours, heaviest month December (20 hours). Add 30 hours for transplanting if starting in frames.

Margin per hour worked: £1

Costs and returns per 1,000 sq ft: sprays

Revenue—3,800 sprays @ 6p	£240	
Less commission @ 10%	24	
		£216
Less crop expenses:		
Cuttings—4,300 @ £20/1,000		90
Fertiliser (as for single-stem crop)		1
Sprays—as required		1
Netting (as for single-stem crop)		1
Fuel (as for single-stem crop)		20
Packaging—170 @ 10p		17
Carriage—170 @ 5p		8
		£138

Margin per 1,000sq ft: £78

Labour requirement: 70 hours, heaviest month December (20 hours).

Margin per hour worked: £1.10

CHRYSANTHEMUMS—lifted crop

Culture: cuttings taken from over-wintered stock are rooted at 60–65°F (15·6–18·3°C) in peat/sand mix or soil/peat blocks during January and February. Rooting can also be accomplished in boxes. When rooted, keep cool and place pots or blocks or line out in frames in March, hardening off for planting out April/May according to region, into well-prepared ground with a pH of 6·5. Dress with 6–8oz general fertiliser per sq yd (12–15cwt per acre). Plant out at 12 x 14in apart in 4–5ft beds. Support with individual canes to facilitate lifting. 'Lifters' can also be grown in 8in pots or 9in whalehide pots using John Innes no 3 potting compost. Regular watering and feeding are essential. Plants are housed in September, either being planted tightly in rows 12–15in apart and well watered in, or placed in pots at convenient spacing. Grow cool.

Target yield: 3 blooms per plant, 1,300 plants per 1,000 sq ft = 3,900 blooms per 1,000sq ft.

Packaging: cardboard boxes lined with paper, 6 blooms per bunch, average 5 bunches per box.

Other facilities: frame space—200sq ft—March/April

Land $\frac{1}{10}$th acre—May–September

Costs and returns per 1,000sq ft

Revenue—650 bunches @ 35p	£227	
Less commission @ 10%	23	
		£204
Less crop expenses:		
Cuttings (replacement 10%) 130 @ £20/1,000		3
Fuel oil—210gals @ 7p		15
Fertiliser		10
Sprays—as required		3
Packaging—130 @ 10p		13
Carriage—130 @ 5p		7
		£51

Margin per 1,000sq ft: £153

Labour requirement: 227 hours, heaviest months September (37 hours), November (36 hours).

Margin per hour worked: £0.67

Pot Plants

AZALEA INDICA

Culture: azaleas for the Christmas market should be bought in September and potted up in 4–6in pots depending on size. Soak the roots well before planting.

Temperature: minimum of 45°F (7·2°C) until the end of September, then step up gradually to 60°F (15·6°C) until flowering, when temperature should be reduced to 55°F (12·8°C).

Production from 1,000sq ft: depending on size of plant, production will be as follows:

	Small	Medium	Large
No of pots per 1,000sq ft (800sq ft bench area)	2,000	800	500
Less wastage 10%	200	80	50
Total production from 1,000sq ft	1,800	720	450

Packaging: cardboard boxes, pots individually wrapped, 8, 6 or 5 pots per crate according to size.

Cost and returns per 1,000sq ft

	Small		Medium		Large	
Revenue	1,800 @ 50p	£900	720 @ £1.2	£864	450 @ £1.7	£765
Less commission @ 10%		90		86		76
		£810		£778		£689
Less crop expenses:						
Plants	2,000 @ 27p	£540	800 @ 50p	£400	500 @ £1	£500

147

	Small		Medium		Large	
Pots	2,000 @ 1p	20	800 @ 1½p	12	500 @ 2p	10
Compost	1.8cu yd @		0.9cu yd @		1cu yd @	
	£5.5/cu yd	10	£5.5/cu yd	5	£5.5/cu yd	6
Fuel oil						
35 secol	450 @ 8p	36	450 @ 8p	36	450 @ 8p	36
Packaging	225 @ 8½p	19	120 @ 8½p	10	90 @ 8½p	8
Carriage	225 @ 5p	11	120 @ 5p	6	90 @ 5p	4
		£636		£469		£564
Margin per 1,000sq ft:	£174			£309		£125

Labour requirement: *small,* 286 hours, heaviest months December (88 hours), September (62 hours); *medium,* 114 hours, heaviest months December (35 hours), September (25 hours); *large,* 72 hours, heaviest months December (22 hours), September (16 hours).

Margin per hour worked: small £0.61, medium £2.71, large £1.74

POT CHRYSANTHEMUMS—Christmas market

Culture: 5 cuttings inserted in September in 5in half-pots in peat/sand compost, placed on benches.

Spacing schedule: 1 week at 6 × 6in
                       2 weeks at 9 × 8in
                       remainder at 12 × 12in

Temperature: minimum of 60°F (15·6°C).

Water: ¼ pint per pot per day.

Production: 750 pots per 1,000sq ft at final spacing.

Target yield: production 750 pots
           Less wastage 5%   38
           Target yield   712 pots

Packaging: plants wrapped in cellophane sleeve and packed in cardboard box (6 pots per box).

Costs and returns per 1,000sq ft

Revenue—712 pots @ 30p	£214	
Less commission @ 10%	21	
		£193
Less crop expenses:		
Cuttings—3,750 @ £20/1,000		75
Fuel oil—650gal @ 7p		45
Pots—750 @ £22/1,000		17
Compost—0·85cu yd @ £6/cu yd		5
Sprays—as required		3
Packaging—119 boxes @ 15p		18
712 sleeves @ £8/1,000		6
Carriage—119 boxes @ 5p		6
		£175

Margin per 1,000sq ft: £18

Labour requirement: 175 hours, heaviest month September (50 hours).

Margin per hour worked: £0.10

POT CHRYSANTHEMUMS—all-year-round

Culture: continuous production throughout the year, based on a programme obtainable from firms which supply the cuttings. Mobile benches give a higher percentage of utilised space than fixed benches, and are recommended for this crop. Artificial lighting and blackout are also required. Four cuttings per pot are required in the summer, compared with five in the winter. Otherwise culture treatment is the same as for the Christmas crop.

Production: with mobile benches—glasshouse area used = 90%

Average bench space per pot = 0·9sq ft

Average number of crops per year = 4

Total production per 1,000sq ft = 900 × 0·9 × 4

= 3,240 pots per year.

Target yield: Total production 3,240 pots
           Less wastage 5%   162
        Target yield   3,078 pots

Packaging: plants wrapped individually in cellophane sleeve and packed in cardboard box (6 pots per box).

Costs and returns per 1,000 sq ft

Revenue—3,078 pots @ 30p	£923	
Less commission @ 10%	92	
		£831
Less crop expenses:		
Cuttings—15,000 @ £18/1,000		270
Fuel oil—2,500 gal @ 7p		175
Pots—3,240 @ £22/1,000		71
Compost—4 cu yd @ £6/cu yd		24
Sprays—as required		20
Electricity, lighting		2
Packaging—513 @ 15p		77
3,078 sleeves @ £8/1,000		25
Carriage—513 @ 5p		26
		£690

Margin per 1,000 sq ft: £141
Labour requirement: 13 hours per week = 650 hours per year.
Margin per hour worked: £0.22

CINERARIAS

Culture: sown in June in seed trays using seed compost. Pricked off in late July into boxes. Potted up in early September for sale at Christmas.

Temperature: 50°F (10°C).

Production from 1,000 sq ft: from 800 sq ft of bench area at final spacing of one pot per sq ft 800 pots
           Less wastage 10%   80

                    720 pots

Packaging: cardboard boxes, 8 pots per box. Pots individually wrapped.

Costs and returns per 1,000sq ft

Revenue—720 @ 25p	£180	
Less commission @ 10%	18	
		£162
Less crop expenses:		
Seed		2
Compost—1½cu yd @ £5.5		8
Seed trays—25 @ 1½p		1
Pots—800 @ 1¼p		10
Fuel oil 35sec—400 @ 8p		32
Sprays, fertilisers etc		2
Packaging—90 @ 12½p		11
Carriage—90 @ 5p		5
		£71

Margin per 1,000sq ft: £91

Labour requirement: 123 hours, heaviest months December (38 hours), September (31 hours).

Margin per hour worked: £0.74

CYCLAMEN

Culture: sow August to October in seed trays using seed compost. Put out into seed boxes (35 plants per box) three weeks after germination. Pot into 5in pots February/March. For sale September–Christmas.

Temperature: 75°F (23·9°C) during germination and then drop to 60–65°F (15·6–18·3°C) until potted up. Thereafter drop to 55°F (12·8°C) until crop is sold.

Production from 1,000sq ft: assuming bench area of 800sq ft
at spacing of one pot per sq ft   800 pots
                    Less wastage 10%   80
                                        ─────
                    Total production   720 pots

Packaging: cardboard boxes, 6 pots per box, pots individually wrapped.

Costs and returns per 1,000sq ft
Revenue—720 pots @ 45p   £324
Less commission @ 10%   32
Less crop expenses: ─────   £292
    Seed—$\frac{1}{3}$oz @ £2/oz   1
    Compost—3cu yd @ £5.5   17
    Pots—800 @ 1$\frac{1}{2}$p   12
    Sprays, liquid feed   12
    Fuel oil, 35sec.—700 @ 8p   56
    Boxes—25 @ 1$\frac{1}{2}$p   1
    Packaging—120 boxes @ 10p   12
    Carriage—120 boxes @ 5p   6
                                                          ─────
                                                          £117

Margin per 1,000sq ft: £175

Labour requirement: 198 hours, heaviest months December (41 hours), June (26 hours).

Margin per hour worked: £0.88

PELARGONIUMS AND GERANIUMS

Culture: cuttings taken from stock plants from August are
trimmed, treated with rooting powder and inserted into 1$\frac{1}{2}$in
peat pots. Pots are placed on benches with bottom heat. Pot

up into 3½in pots for sale in January/February, or 4in pots for sale in March/April.

Temperature: minimum of 50°F (10°C).

Production from 1,000sq ft: assuming bench area of 800sq ft, approximately 2,200 plants can be produced per 1,000sq ft as follows:

in 3½in pots	30%	660 pots
in 4in pots	60%	1,320 pots
wastage 10%		220 pots

Packaging: cardboard boxes, average 12 pots per box, pots individually wrapped in cellophane sleeve.

Costs and returns per 1,000sq ft

Revenue—660 @ 15p		£ 99	
1,320 @ 20p		264	
		£363	
Less commission @ 10%		36	£327
Less crop expenses:			
Pots—3½ & 4in 2,000 @ £9/1,000			18
Peat pots—2,200 @ £3/1,000			7
Compost—1cu yd @ £5.5			6
Fuel oil, 35sec.—300gal @ 8p			24
Sprays, fertiliser, rooting powder.			
Estimated figure			9
Packaging—165 @ 12½p			21
2,000 sleeves @ £4/1,000			8
Carriage—165 @ 5p			8
			£101

Margin per 1,000sq ft: £226

Labour requirement: 119 hours, heaviest months October (37 hours), April (19 hours).

Margin per hour worked: £1.90

K

POINSETTIAS

Culture: plants for sale at Christmas should be purchased at end of July and potted up in 5in pots filled with compost. Four weeks later they should be sprayed with a growth-regulating hormone such as cycocel.

Temperature: 70°F (21·1°C) for first week, thereafter 65°F (18·3°C) minimum.

Fertiliser: two applications of liquid feed during season.

Spray: against whitefly 3–4 times with Malathion or Parathion.

Production from 1,000sq ft: bench area = 800sq ft, assuming 80% of glasshouse area used, at spacing of 8 × 8in. Bench could take about 1,800 plants. Allowing a 10% wastage this would mean a total of 1,620 saleable plants.

Packaging: cardboard boxes, 8 pots per box. Pots should be individually wrapped.

Costs and returns per 1,000sq ft

Revenue—1,620 @ 35p	£567	
Less commission @ 10%	57	
Less crop expenses:		£510
Plants—1,800 @ £95/1,000		171
Pots—1,800 @ £15/1,000		27
Compost		15
Sprays		21
Fertiliser—liquid feed		5
Fuel oil—35sec oil, 700gal @ 8p		56
Packaging—202 boxes @ 12½p		26
Carriage—202 boxes @ 5p		10
		£331

Margin per 1,000sq ft: £179

Labour requirement: 216 hours, heaviest months December (112 hours), July (40 hours).

Margin per hour worked: £0.83

OTHER POT PLANTS

The range of pot plants which can be grown under glass is enormous and the following are merely some examples of the more popular lines. Calculating production costs and gross margins follows a basically similar pattern to those plants which are covered in the following notes, the most applicable figure for cheaper pot plants being under the short-term foliage plants (see page 156).

Abutilon Insigne Hybridum
Achimenes Mixed Colours
Antirrhinum (dwarf)
Aster Waldersee Mixed
Balsam TT Extra Dwarf Mixed
Begonia Semperflorens Varieties
,, Tuberous Rooted Varieties
Browallia Varieties
Calceolaria Mixtures
Capsicum Varieties
Celosia Plumosa Varieties
Chrysanthemum Charm
,, Coronarium Golden
,, Gem
Cineraria Mixtures *
Clianthus Dampieri
Cornflower isophylla
Cuphea Platycentra
Cyclamen Varieties *
Dianthus Baby Doll
Eucalyptus Citriodora
,, Globulus
Exacum Affine
Geranium Varieties *
Gerbera
Gloxinia

Grevillea Robusta
Heliotropium Marine
Impatiens Varieties
Jacaranda Mimosaefolia
Kalanchoe
Marigold F.1. Carnation Flw. Series
,, F.1. Moonshot
Matricaria Nana Golden Ball
,, ,, Snowball
,, TT White Stars
Mimosa Pudica
Petunia Various Types
Primrose Biedermeier Strain
,, Easter Bouquet
Primula Kewensis
,, Malacoides Varieties
,, Obconica Varieties
,, Sinensis Fimbriata Varieties
,, Stellata Varieties
Rosa Polyantha Fairy Rose
Saintpaulia Varieties
Schizanthus Varieties
Solanum Capsicastrum Nanum
Streptocarpus Hybrids
Vinca Varieties
Zygocactus truncatus

* See Notes that follow.

(*list by courtesy of Asmer Seeds, Leicester*)

Foliage Plants

Culture: the term 'foliage plants' covers a wide range of species with varied propagation methods, both vegetative and from seed. The 'cheaper' range of pot plants includes such items as coleus, pilea, ricinis, tradescantia and saxifraga. Coleus is grown from seed sown at various times of the year, tradescantia and saxifraga from cuttings taken almost anytime, ricinis from seed sown in January/February.

Others are: acalypha, acorus, aralia, aspidistra, ampelopsis, begonias in variety, caladium, chlorophytum, cissus, croton, cordyline, cyperus, dieffenbachia, euonymus, fatshedera, fatzia, ficus, fittonia, grevillea robusta, gynura, hedera (ivies), helexine, maranta, monstera, peperomia, rhoicissus, sansevaria, scindapus, sedum, selaginella, sparmannia.

Production: from all-year-round production approximately 3,000 plants grown in 1,000sq ft of glass, assuming benches occupy 75% of glasshouse area.

Target yield: from 3,000 plants deduct wastage of 5% = 150
Used for stock plants 5%   150
                                                    ─────
                                                      300
                                                    ─────

Target yield per 1,000sq ft = 2,700 plants

Packaging: cardboard boxes, 18 pots per box.

Crop costs and returns per 1,000sq ft

Revenue—2,700 plants @ 12½p	£338	
Less commission @ 10%	34	
		£304
Less crop expenses:		
Seed (eg coleus and begonia rex)		2
Pots—3,000 @ £10/1,000		30
Compost—3cu yd @ £6/cu yd		18
Boxes (depreciation)		3
Sprays—as required		6
Fuel oil—1,500gal @ 7p		105
Packaging—150 @ 15p		23
Carriage—150 @ 5p		8
		£195

Margin per 1,000sq ft: £109

Labour requirement: approximately 3 hours per week = 150 hours per year.

Margin per hour worked: £0.73

Bedding Plants

In constant demand in most areas, but specialised production techniques are gradually being introduced.

Culture: sow mid-January onwards in boxes using soil-less compost. 500 plants per box. Temperature 65°F (18·3°C) for 2–3 weeks. Pelleted seed is now available for some plants, and reduces costs considerably.

Pricking out: into fish boxes or plastic trays, soil or peat blocks, or break-up containers, using potting compost. Traditionally 4doz plants per box but smaller containers can be used depending on the needs of the market. Soil blocks now becoming popular. Decimalisation may also mean planting in tens. Temperature 50–60°F (10–15·6°C) for 3–4 weeks.

The modern technique of using growing rooms for bedding-plant culture has many advantages, full details of this being obtainable from the Electricity Boards' booklets.

Hardening off: transfer to frames until ready for sale in a few weeks time. Plastic structures are being used effectively for bedding plants.

Sprays: as required.

Production from 1,000sq ft

Efficiency factors	Target	Output per 1,000sq ft
% usable floor area	100%	1,000sq ft
% occupied floor area	80%	800sq ft
% working area	20%	200sq ft
No boxes/sq ft floor area occupied	1 box/sq ft	800 boxes

Efficiency factors — *Target* — *Output per 1,000sq ft*

No of plants per box	50	40,000 plants
No of batches per season (Jan–June)	3	2,400 boxes × 50 plants = 120,000 plants
% wastage	15%	400 boxes
No of boxes marketed	85%	2,000 boxes × 50 plants

Period glass occupied: varies with (a) variety of plant; (b) season of year—1 day in April having about same 'growing power' as 2 days in January/February.

Approx dates	*Batch 1*	*Batch 2*	*Batch 3*
Sown	Mid-Jan	1st week March	2nd week April
Pricked off	1st week Feb.	3rd week March	3rd week April
Hardened off	2nd week Mar.	2nd week April	2nd week May
Sold	April	May	June

Average length of time occupied

	Batch 1	*Batch 2*	*Batch 3*
Sown—pricked off	20 days	15 days	10 days
Pricked off—hardened off	35 days	20 days	20 days
Total	55 days	35 days	30 days

Seedling production in growing rooms (from Growing Room Handbook No 1—Electricity Council)

Variety	*Period (days)*	*Variety*	*Period (days)*
French Marigold	2	Alyssum	6
Aster	3	Antirrhinum	7
Stocks	3	Phlox	7
Mesembryanthemum	5	Salvia	7
Petunia	5	Lobelia	10
		Begonia Semperflorens	14

Method of sale: direct to shops or retail (retail price 70p —shop price 50p).

Costs and returns per 1,000sq ft

Revenue—2,000 boxes @ 50p	£1,000
Less crop expenses:	
Seed, cuttings	18
Compost—13½cu yd @ £6.5	86
Fuel oil—650gal @ 8p	52
Boxes—2,000 @ 3p	60
Water—sprays, etc	1
	£217

Margin per 1,000sq ft: £783

Labour requirement—800 boxes

Job	Rate of Work	No of units	Total hours
Fill seed boxes and sow seed	10 boxes/hour	80 boxes	8
Spray, water, etc		100sq ft	4
Prick off, fill and carry boxes	6 boxes/hour	800 boxes	133
Water, spray, etc		1,000sq ft	16
Transfer to frames	12 boxes/hour	800 boxes	67
Water, uncover & cover frames		170 × 5ft	48
			276

Total labour requirement: 1st batch, 276 hours, heaviest month February (143 hours); 2nd batch, 276 hours, heaviest month March (149 hours); 3rd batch, 276 hours, heaviest month April (149 hours).

Margin per hour worked: £0.95

Note: see page 73 on capital costs and depreciation.

SPRING BEDDING PLANTS

The growing of wallflowers, as polyanthus (and other plants), for sale in the autumn has a limited but constant appeal. Wallflowers can be space sown (using pelleted seed) in boxes.

Cut Flowers

Out of doors
Variable demands according to area.

BULBS & CORMS

Anemones

Culture: plant corms 4in apart and 2–3in deep in rows 20–24in apart in well-prepared ground dressed with farmyard manure and organic fertiliser at 5–6oz per sq yd (10cwt per acre). Planting time varies according to region and can commence in April, proceeding until August, when flowers are produced well into the winter. Some protection will assist with extended flowering.

Target yield: 20,000 bunches per acre.

Packaging: cardboard flower-boxes, 15 bunches per box.

Costs and returns per acre

Revenue—20,000 bunches @ 5p	£1,000	
Less commission @ 10%	100	
		£900
Less crop expenses:		
Corms—80,000 @ 60p/1,000		48
Fertiliser		45
Sprays—as required		4
Packaging—1,333 boxes @ 8p		107
Carriage—1,333 boxes @ 5p		67
		£271

Margin per acre: £629

Labour requirement: 1,217 hours, heaviest months October (360 hours), September (270 hours).

Margin per hour worked: £0.52

Daffodils

Culture: cutting can vary over a wide period according to region and site. Protection can induce much earlier flowering. Planting double-nozed bulbs takes place in well-prepared beds in September/October, 5in deep, bulb to bulb, in 4–5ft beds; rows 10–12in apart. The application of CIPC weedkiller is essential to avoid hand-labour of weeding.

Planted per acre: 7 tons.

Target yield per ton: 18,000 blooms.

Production per acre: 126,000 blooms or 12,600 bunches × 10.

Packaging: cardboard boxes—24 bunches per box.

Cost of establishment per acre

Bulbs—7 tons @ £130	£910
Farmyard manure—20 tons @ £1.5	30
Sprays—as required	6
	£946

Labour requirement, for establishment (in hours): preparing ground, 14; planting, 140; spraying, 4; total 158 hours.

Annual costs and returns per acre

Revenue—12,600 @ 4p	£504	
Less commission @ 10%	50	
Less crop expenses:		£454
Share of establishment (excluding bulbs)		4
Fertiliser		8
Sprays—as required		6
Packaging—525 @ 10p		53
Carriage—525 @ 5p		26
		£97

Margin per acre: £357

Labour requirement: mainly cutting in April/May, 450 hours; share of establishment, 16 hours; total 466 hours.

Margin per hour worked: £0.76

Note: at the end of two years the bulbs may be lifted, by which time the weight of bulbs may be $1\frac{1}{2}$–$2\frac{1}{2}$ times that originally planted. The additional bulbs may be sold, treated for forcing, or simply used to extend the area of outdoor cropping.

Tulips

Culture: as for daffodils, but depth of planting should be 4in in this case.

Quantity planted per acre: 200,000.

Target yield: flowers cut—80%.

Production per acre: 160,000 blooms or 27,000 bunches × 6.

Cost of establishment per acre

Bulbs 200,000 @ £14/1,000	£2,800	
Farmyard manure—20 tons @ £1.5	30	
Sprays—as required	6	
	£2,836	

Labour requirement, for establishment per acre: preparing the ground, 14 hours; planting (mainly July), 413 hours; spraying, 4 hours; total 431 hours.

Annual costs and returns per acre

Revenue—27,000 @ 3.3p	£900	
Less commission @ 10%	90	
		£810
Less crop expenses:		
Share of establishment (excluding bulbs)		4
Fertiliser		8
Sprays—as required		6
Packaging—1,700 @ 10p		170
Carriage—1,700 @ 5p		85
		£273

Margin per acre: £537

Labour requirement: cutting—May/June, 630 hours; share of establishment (July), 43 hours; total 673 hours.

Margin per hour worked: £0.80

Note: Bottom leaf should not be cut so that bulbs will be re-usable the following season. Ideally, bulbs should be lifted each year, yielding 2 additional bulbs (10/11cm) which may be planted out and grown on until of saleable size. Alternatively they may be heat-treated for forcing.

ASTERS

Culture: seed is sown in February/March, being pricked out in soil or peat blocks or boxes, hardening off for planting out in well-prepared ground in April/May at a distance of 12 × 12in apart in 4–5ft wide beds and cutting in July/August.

Target yield: 30,000 bunches (× 12).

Packaging: cardboard flower-boxes—24 bunches per box.

Costs and returns per acre

Revenue—30,000 bunches @ 4p	£1,200	
Less commission @ 10%	120	
Less crop expenses:		£1,080
Seed—3lb @ £15/lb		45
Fertiliser—4cwt compound @ £2.9		12
Sprays—as required		10
Packaging—1,250 boxes @ 10p		125
Carriage—1,250 boxes @ 5p		63
		£255

Margin per acre: £825

Labour requirement: 1,518 hours, heaviest months July (600 hours), August (600 hours).

Margin per hour worked: £0.55

CHRYSANTHEMUMS

Culture: similar to that for lifters, see page 145. Harvested August–October (part under sashes).

Target yield: 8,500 bunches × 6.

Packaging: cardboard flower-boxes, average 5 bunches per box.

Crop costs and returns per acre

Revenue—8,500 bunches @ 25p	£2,125	
Less commission @ 10%	213	
		£1,912
Less crop expenses:		
Cuttings (replacement 10%) 400 @ £20/1,000		8
Fertiliser—10cwt compound @ £3		30
Sprays—as required		20
Canes (replacement)		40
Packaging—1,700 @ 10p		170
Carriage—1,700 @ 5p		85
		£353

Margin per acre—£1,559

Labour requirement: 1,970 hours, heaviest months September (350 hours), October (350 hours).

Margin per hour worked: £0.79

DAHLIAS

Culture: dahlias are produced from cuttings taken from over-wintered tubers (the tubers themselves can also be planted out to give an earlier flower). Cuttings are induced to form by bedding the tubers in moist peat at 60°F (15·6°C) and rooting selected cuttings in Jiffy 7s or peat blocks during February. Lay plants on a mulch of peat when rooted or put in 3in pots and harden off in frame. Plant out in May at 2 x 2ft apart in beds 5ft wide or on a 2½ft square system. Support with sticks or steel wires or netting. Cutting commences according to season and is finished by frost. Dahlias can also be produced much earlier and later by planting in plastic structures or in vacant greenhouses. A frequent practice is to inter-plant a lettuce crop with dahlia tubers.

Target yield: 20,000 bunches.

Packaging: cardboard flower-boxes, 20 bunches per box.

Crop costs and returns per acre

Revenue—2,000 bunches @ 60p	£1,200	
Less commission @ 10%	120	
		£1,080
Less crop expenses:		
Tubers (replacement)		144
Fertiliser—10cwt @ £3		30
Pots, compost		50
Sprays—as required		8
Stakes and wire netting (replacement)		40
Packaging—1,000 boxes @ 10p		100
Carriage—1,000 boxes @ 5p		50
		£422

Margin per acre: £658

Labour requirement: 1,910 hours, heaviest months October (335 hours), July, August and September (300 hours each).

Margin per hour worked: £0.34

PYRETHRUMS

Culture: a very useful and popular crop which can remain in production for some years. Propagation is by division of established plants in July after flowering, planting up in 4–5ft wide beds at 15 × 15in apart in well-manured plots. Beds can remain productive for some years by forking in well-rotted farmyard manure in February, coupled with a 4–5oz per sq yd compound fertiliser in spring. Slugs can be troublesome, especially in winter, necessitating preventive measures.

Target yield: 12,000 bunches × 12.

Packaging: cardboard flower-boxes, 36 bunches per box.

Crop costs and returns per acre

Revenue—12,000 bunches @ 6p	£720	
Less commission @ 10%	72	
		£648
Less crop expenses:		
Stock plants (replacement)		60
Fertiliser—10cwt compound @ £3		30
Sprays—as required		10
Packaging—330 boxes @ 10p		33
Carriage—330 boxes @ 5p		17
		£150

Margin per acre: £498

Labour requirement: 465 hours, heaviest month June (250 hours).

Margin per hour worked: £1.07

STOCKS

Culture: raised from seed sown in February/March in boxes and pricked out in soil blocks (selecting doubles), planting out in April/May at 8 × 8in in 4–5ft beds in ground dressed with 4oz per sq yd of general fertiliser and with a pH of 6·5.

Target yield: 7,000 bunches × 6.

Packaging: cardboard flower-boxes, 8 bunches per box.

Costs and returns per acre

Revenue—7,000 bunches @ 23p	£1,610	
Less commission @ 10%	161	
Less crop expenses:	——	£1,449
Seed—3lb @ £48		144
Fertiliser—10cwt compound @ £3		30
Sprays—as required		10
Packaging—875 boxes @ 8p		70
Carriage—875 boxes @ 5p		44
		———
		£298

Margin per acre: £1,151

Labour requirement: 754 hours, heaviest months July (170 hours), April (155 hours).

Margin per hour worked: £1.53

SWEET PEAS

Can be a useful source of income.

Culture: seed sown in January. Plant out in April in cordon or hedge fashion on tall supports.

No accurate economic figures available

SWEET WILLIAM

Culture: a perennial treated as a biennial, sown in May/June in seed bed and pricked off at 9 × 9in for planting in September to flower the following May. Ground should be treated with 4oz per sq yd of general fertiliser.

Target yield: 30,000 bunches.

Packaging: cardboard flower-boxes, 18 bunches per box.

Costs and returns per acre

Revenue—30,000 bunches @ 5p	£1,500	
Less commission @ 10%	150	
		£1,350
Less crop expenses:		
Seed—1½lb @ £6	9	
Fertiliser—10cwt compound @ £3	30	
Sprays—as required	10	
Packaging—1,667 boxes @ 8p	133	
Carriage—1,667 boxes @ 5p	83	
	£265	

Margin per acre: £1,085

Labour requirement: 1,775 hours, heaviest months June (802 hours), May (702 hours).

Margin per hour worked: £0.61

CARNATIONS (under glass)

Culture: plants can be grown in raised beds 4–5ft wide or in 9in pots. Plant at various times of the year at 6 × 6in. Pinch to encourage side growth and thereafter pinch, feed and water regularly. Success depends on regular supplies of quality blooms over a major part of the year. Ventilation is essential to avoid fungal disorders.

Life of crop: cuttings bought in March or April grown on for 18–21 months.

Spacing: 6 × 6in = 2,800 per 1,000sq ft using 70% of floor area.

Temperature: minimum of 50°F (10°C).

Supplementary lighting: tungsten filament lamps. 100 watt lamps at 6ft intervals for 6 weeks from 1 August and again in February.

L

Staking: stakes with nets every 6in up to a height of 6ft.
Fertiliser: as for tomatoes.
Packaging: cardboard boxes—80 flowers per box.
Yield: 20,000 stems per 1,000sq ft or approximately 8 per plant.
Grading: 1st grade 60%; 2nd grade 40%.
Equipment: modern glasshouse.

Crop costs and returns per 1,000sq ft

			Total	Per Yr
Revenue— 600 doz @ 30p ⎫			£680	£340
1,000 doz @ 50p ⎭				
Less crop expenses:		£		
Cuttings, estimated cost		100		
Fuel—heating, 1,700 @ 5p		85		
sterilisation		3		
Electricity—heat'g @ 10% of oil cost		9		
lighting		1		
Netting—(over 7 years)				
1,200sq yd @ 8p		14		
Fertiliser, estimated cost		17		
Packaging—625 @ 10p		63		
Carriage—625 @ 5p		32	£324	£162
			£356	£178
Margin per 1,000sq ft:			£170	£ 85

FREESIA

Culture: sow seed in boxes of moist peat covered with paper and glass in November. Pinch out 2in apart in 9in whalehide pots in John Innes no 2 or soil-less compost. Stand pots outside in June and bring into greenhouse in September and keep cool (50°F—10°C). Support with twigs will be necessary.
Target yield: 4,000 bunches per 1,000sq ft.
Packaging: cardboard boxes, 24 bunches per box.

Crop costs and returns per 1,000sq ft

Revenue—4,000 bunches @ 12p	£480	
Less commission @ 10%	48	
		£432
Less crop expenses:		
Seed—12oz @ £6 per oz	72	
Pots—1,500 @ £13/1,000	20	
Compost—10 tons @ £10	100	
Fertiliser—1¼cwt @ £9	11	
Fuel—300gal @ 8p	24	
Sprays, etc—as required	4	
Packaging—167 @ 8p	13	
Carriage—167 @ 4p	7	
	£251	

Margin per 1,000sq ft: £181

Labour requirement: 288 hours, heaviest months November (79 hours), December (72 hours).

Margin per hour worked: £0.63

ROSES (under glass)

Rose-growing under glass is a specialised task demanding strict attention to detail. While roses can be grown in pots, they are best grown in 4–5ft wide beds, planted 10 × 10in apart, with a minimum temperature of 50°F (10°C), coupled with regular trimming and pruning as necessary. They require constant vigilance against pests and diseases, particularly mildew. This can be a lucrative crop if quality is high.

Temperature: 'low regime'—55°F (12·8°C) night, 65°F (18·3°C) day. No heating July or August.

Carbon dioxide: 20lb per acre per hour from 1 February until mid-April, and 1 October till 14 December.

Spacing: grafts are spaced at 12 × 12in = 750 per 1,000sq ft, using 75% of floor space.

Fertiliser: 14oz potassium nitrate ⎫ per 200gal water with
            10oz urea   ⎬ every other watering.
            lime added to maintain pH of 6–6.5.

Sprays: as required against red spider mite and mildew.

Yield: 1st year 7 blooms per plant = 5,250 blooms per 1,000 sq ft.
      Following years 15 blooms per plant = 11,250.
      Average over 10 years = 10,650 blooms or 887 bunches × 12.

Packaging: cardboard boxes.

Equipment: modern glasshouse.

Costs and returns per 1,000sq ft
Revenue—887doz @ 50p   £444
Less crop expenses:

Grafts (depreciation over 10 years)—		
750 @ £140 per 1,000	£11	
Fuel oil—1,800gal @ 8p	144	
Carbon dioxide—900lb @ 1½p	14	
Fertiliser, estimated cost	4	
Sprays, estimated cost	2	
Packaging—450 @ 10p	45	
Carriage—450 @ 5p	23	243

Gross margin per 1,000sq ft: £201

OTHER FLOWERS UNDER GLASS

The following flowers are also frequently grown under glass for cut blooms:

Antirrhinums: tall F1 American variety.

Stocks (100% double).

Gypsophila (annual).

Sweet peas.

All are seed-raised and planted out in greenhouse borders in

February–April, according to level of heat available. Returns can be very variable according to demand.

ORCHIDS

While orchids tend to be a specialised crop, they can be an extremely useful and lucrative source of income as cut blooms on a smaller scale, concentrating on the hardy types such as Cypripedium and others.

Mushrooms

Mushrooms can be a worthwhile crop if intelligently handled and if there is a cellar or well-insulated outhouse or garage available. They can be a very temperamental crop demanding strict attention to detail and a high labour content, when grown on a small scale; this tends to make them less lucrative than appears at first sight. A number of firms sell spawn and other material for mushroom growing and also help with marketing. Experience shows that the 'calamity' rate is high and a succession of enthusiasts start off well, becoming less enthusiastic eventually, but in fairness this can also be said of many other facets of horticulture.

Ideally a readily available supply of horse manure or straw to make the compost is essential if mushrooms are to be grown on a commercial scale. Some form of heating will also be required, although summer cropping is effective without heat.

Buildings must be scrupulously clean and properly ventilated to avoid high humidities. Darkness is preferable but not vital, but obviously better insulation can be achieved in solid buildings.

Culture
Mushrooms today tend to be grown on a large factory scale with every possible facet of culture carried out mechanically. They can be grown in beds, but 3 × 2ft stacking trays make best use of available space. For timing allow a period of 6–8 weeks after spawning before cropping begins, which should

then extend for 3–4 months. Strawy horse manure is stacked in 4–5ft square heaps not more than 5ft high; they are soaked thoroughly using a mild antiseptic such as Lysol (one teaspoon per gallon) in the water. Turn after 7–8 days and add more water if necessary, turning a total of 4–5 times. Alternatively straw and special compost makers can be used following instructions supplied with the compost maker. Beds are made up from the compost 4ft wide and 9–10in deep in summer, 12–15in in winter, or 8in deep in trays. Beds can also be made up out of doors in a ridge form 30in wide, tapering to 6in or so, at a height of 24in. Allow ventilation for a few days after making up beds or filling trays in a building, and when compost temperature drops to 70–75°F (21·1–23·9°C), insert spawn every 10in according to suppliers' instructions.

In 7–9 days when the mycelium can be seen developing from the spawn, cover with a 1–2in layer of peat with ground limestone added at approximately $1\frac{1}{2}$–2lb per bushel to render it alkaline. Beds are kept dry at first, then very well watered, and mushrooms will appear according to temperature.

Very strict attention must be given to management and any pest attack dealt with immediately. Diseases, when they occur, can be disastrous, as conditions for their development are of course ideal, and can wipe out the whole crop. Prospective growers are urged to obtain full details from suppliers of spawn, there being a wealth of information available.

Production per 1,000sq ft of shed

	Target	Output/1,000sq ft
Floor area occupied	65%	650sq ft
No of tiers	4	2,600sq ft bed area
Yield per sq ft of bed area	3lb	7,800lb

Packaging: cardboard baskets—3lb per basket.

Crop costs and returns per 1,000sq ft

Revenue—2,500 baskets @ 65p	£1,625	
Less commission @ 10%	163	
Less crop expenses:		£1,462
Spawn—estimated cost		60
Compost—10 bags poultry manure @ £2		20
Gypsum, activator, fertiliser, sprays		25
Straw—20cwt @ 35p/cwt		7
Peat		40
Fuel—2,400gal @ 8p		192
Packaging—2,600 @ 4p		104
Carriage—2,600 @ 4p		104
		£552

Margin per 1,000sq ft: £969
Labour requirement: 25 hours/week = 1,250 hours per year.
Margin per hour worked: £0.78

Nursery Stock Production

The nursery-stock industry has seen many changes during the past ten years, having grown from a position of relative insignificance to become a sector of major importance within the horticultural industry. With the emphasis on 'do-it-yourself' gardening, the garden centre has emerged as a major retail outlet for all forms of nursery stock with selling organised on the lines of a food supermarket. To satisfy the market it has set out to supply everything a gardener needs, including plants, fertilisers and garden tools.

The primary cause of this change has been the tremendous increase in demand for garden plants and materials. This increased demand may be attributed to the increased use of nursery stock for private and rented house gardens, industrial estates, motorways and recreational areas. A garden can be as much a status symbol as a car or a colour television, and the number and quality of landscape features is often the only outward manifestation of the social position of the family in the community. At a more mercenary level the effect on property values of establishing an attractive garden has also been an important factor. This applies particularly to new houses, where money spent on the garden must be considered as one of the best ways for a young couple to increase the value of what is probably the biggest asset they will ever own.

Yet another factor contributing to the increasing demand for nursery stock has been the recent emphasis of both public authorities and private developers on the need to preserve the environment. The increasing awareness of the importance of landscaping housing areas and industrial developments is recognised now as a means of creating the kind of physical and social environment in which people want to live and work.

While present trends indicate that the nursery-stock industry can expect continual growth and expansion, success in this highly competitive business depends on a sound knowledge of plants, their methods of propagation and training, proper management and the ability to provide the kind of gardening service needed to develop good customer relations. There is much to be said for a co-operative approach to publicity, as operated by Dutch and Belgian nurseries.

PROPAGATION OF TREES AND SHRUBS

Undoubtedly the easiest way to start is with the cheaper range of trees and shrubs which are fairly easy to raise from cuttings or seed, concentrating on varieties which grow well in the district concerned; since the production of good-quality plants is the first essential. Having said that it must also be pointed out that anything which is easy to grow is usually less lucrative, items which are difficult or expensive to grow will invariably make a bigger profit. Few people, however, seem to be aware of just how easy it is to strike cuttings of many popular shrubs such as forsythia, weigellia and hebes. Others, such as cotoneaster and brooms, can be just as easily raised from seed.

In general, propagation from seed is less satisfactory than vegetative methods such as cuttings, layering or simple division, since it is seldom possible to reproduce exactly the type of plant required. As it is desirable to produce named varieties of shrubs, vegetative methods are more commonly used in commercial practice. Seed propagation, however, is a useful and cheap method of increasing the range of stock carried by introducing new varieties and is used exclusively for many hard and softwood trees.

Outdoor Rooting of Cuttings

Cuttings are taken from stock plants, trimmed and treated with hormone powder. These are inserted in the open ground in the spring or autumn. Sand and peat may be forked into the ground to improve the condition of the soil. This is also a very cheap method of propagating shrubs, but the percentage of cuttings which root may be fairly low and rooting may take anything up to a year.

Approximate cost per 1,000 cuttings

	£
Hormone powder—100g @ £3/1,000	0.30
Peat and sand—estimated cost	1.00
Labour—6½ hours @ 60p	3.90
	£5.20

Labour requirement and cost per 1,000 cuttings

Job	Rate of work	No of cuttings	Total hours	Rate/ hour	Total Cost
				p	£
Preparation of ground	30min/1,000 cuttings	1,000	0.5	60	0.30
Preparing & inserting cuttings	170/hour	1,000	6.0	60	3.60
			6.5		£3.90

Cuttings rooted: 50%
Cost per 1,000 rooted cuttings produced: £10.40
These costings do not include the cost or upkeep of stock plants.

Rooting of Cuttings in Cold Frames or Plastic Tunnels

Cuttings are taken from stock plants as before, trimmed and treated with hormone powder. They are then inserted in a bed containing a rooting medium of sand and/or peat—softwood cuttings in a sandy soil early in the growing season; hardwood cuttings in a sand/peat mixture in the autumn. An additional covering of light opaque plastic sheeting gives better results and is particularly desirable for more difficult subjects.

A wider range of shrub species can be propagated by this method than growing outdoors. Quicker rooting species such as forsythia, hypericum, escallonia, are less critical as far as date of planting is concerned than the slower rooting items. Because of this a strict timetable should be followed for the slower varieties, filling in with the quicker rooting species when there is space available. Rooting percentages may range from 100% in 1–2 months for the quicker rooting items to 50% in 6–8 months for the more difficult subjects.

Space utilisation and output per 1,000sq ft

	Efficiency factors	Target	Output per year
1	Usable floor area	100%	1,000sq ft
2	Floor area occupied	80%	800sq ft
3	Working area	20%	200sq ft
4	Cuttings/sq ft floor area occupied*	36	28,800 cuttings
5	Batches per year (average)	2	57,600 cuttings
6	Cuttings rooted (average)	60%	34,500 cuttings

Cost per 1,000sq ft

	£
Cuttings—57,600 (see below)	–
Hormone powder—5,000gm @ £3/1,000	15
Peat—55cu yd or 19 ton @ £7	133
Sand—55cu yd or 55 ton @ 60p	33
Polythene sheeting @ £5/1,000sq ft	5
Labour—525 hours @ 60p	315
Share of capital cost (plastic tunnel)	25
	£526

Cost of 1,000 rooted cuttings: £15.20

*Density varies greatly.

These figures do not include the cost of stock plants or obtaining cuttings, obviously a variable which must be taken into account.

Labour requirement and cost per 1,000sq ft

Job	Rate of work	No of units	Total hours	Rate/ hour p	Total Cost £
Preparation of frames	17min/200 cuttings	57,600	82	60	49
Preparation of cuttings	170/hour	57,600	339	60	203
Care of crop	3hrs/1,000 rooted	34,500	104	60	63
			525		£315

Capital costs

		Total cost	Life	Annual Cost
Plastic tunnel—structure	5p/sq ft	£50	10yrs	£ 5
cladding—	4p/sq ft	£40	2yrs	£20
				£25
Frames—	12p/sq ft	£120	8yrs	£15

Rooting of Cuttings in a Mist Unit Under Heated Glass
  (see appendix)
Prepared cuttings are inserted in pots or containers and placed in a mist unit. Soil warming to a temperature of 70–75°F (21·1–23·9°C) is desirable for quick rooting, and can be achieved by means of thermostatically controlled electric cables with a loading of 15 watts per sq ft or hot-water mini-bore systems. Since an artificial environment is created using this equipment, timing is less critical and many cuttings can be produced throughout the year. Again careful programming is necessary in order to make best use of the space available. Quick-rooting subjects should be propagated separately from those slower to root. On average 70% rooting can be expected within 1–3 months. Opaque polythene is now used with considerable success in lieu of mist units.

Space utilisation and output per 1,000sq ft

	Efficiency Factors	Target	Output per year
1	Usable floor area	100%	1,000sq ft
2	Benched area	80%	800sq ft
3	Working area	20%	200sq ft
4	Cuttings per sq ft bench area	36	28,800 cuttings
5	Batches per year	5	144,000 cuttings
6	Cuttings rooted	70%	100,800 cuttings

Costs per 1,000sq ft

	£
Cuttings—144,000	–
Hormone powder—12,750gm @ £3/1,000	38
Peat—19 ton @ £7	133
Sand—55 ton @ 60p	33
Electricity—86,400 units @ 1p*	864
Fuel—air heating (45°F: 7·2°C) 320gal @ 5p	16
Labour—1,406 hours @ 60p	843
Share of capital cost	171
	£2,098

Cost per 1,000 cuttings rooted: £20.80

Once again stock plants or cuttings are not allowed for.

Labour requirement and cost

Job	Rate of work	No of units	Total hours	Rate/ hour	Total Cost £
Preparing compost and filling containers	700 per hour	144,000	206	60p	123
Preparing and inserting cuttings	170 per hour	144,000	847	60p	508
Care of crop	1 hour/day	65 days	65	60p	39
Transplanting to floor of greenhouse or frames	500/hour	144,000	288	60p	173
			1,406		£843

* Running costs with mini-bore systems will be much lower.

Propagation by Layering

Layering is not a method which readily lends itself to large-scale commercial production. It is nevertheless useful for propagating the more difficult species where sophisticated equipment for rooting cuttings is not available. Items which may be propagated in this way include rhododendrons, acers (maples) and magnolias. There are two methods:

1. Side shoots of stock plants are selected. These are bent, without breaking the stem, the aim being to restrict the flow of sap and so induce rooting. The layer may also be treated with hormone rooting powder before firmly pressing into the soil or rooting medium alongside the stock plant. A stone or peg may be used to hold the layered stem firmly in the ground. With some species three years may elapse before rooting takes place and the layered plant is ready for transplanting.

2. Aerial layering may be used where it is difficult to layer in the soil surrounding the stock plant. The method is as follows: Make two parallel cuts about 1in apart around the stem with a sharp knife. Scrape the bark away from the stem between the two cuts. Wrap a sheet of polythene (taped at each end) containing some rooting medium round stem, and tie tightly. After roots have sprouted the branch is ready for transplanting.

Method 1—approximate costs per 1,000 layers

	£
Hormone powder—100gm @ £3/1,000	0.30
Peat and sand—estimated cost	1.00
Pegs—1,000	0.50
Labour	3.90
Total cost	£5.70

Labour requirement per 1,000 layers

Job	Rate of work	No of units	Total hours	Rate/ hour p	Total Cost £
Preparation of ground	30 min/1,000 layers	1,000	0.5	60	0.30
Preparing & inserting layers	170/hour	1,000	6.0	60	3.60
			6.5		£3.90

Layers rooted: 70%

Cost per 1,000 rooted layers produced: £8.10

Cost of stock plants not included.

Method 2 (air layering)—approximate cost per 1,000 layers

	£
Hormone powder—100gm @ £3/1,000	0.30
Rooting medium—approx 1cu ft @ 25p	0.25
Polythene and ties @ £2/1,000	2.00
Labour—18 hours @ 60p	10.80
Total cost	£13.35

Labour requirement per 1,000 layers

Job	Rate of work	No of units	Total hours	Rate/ hour	Total Cost £
Preparing & trimming cuttings	170/hour	1,000	6	60p	3.60
Wrapping polythene round stem with rooting medium	120/hour	1,000	8	60p	4.80
Transplanting rooted layers	170/hour	700	4	60p	2.40
			18		£10.80

Layers rooted: 70%

Cost per 1,000 rooted layers produced: £19.10

Cost of stock plants not included.

GROWING-ON ROOTED CUTTINGS AND LAYERS

At this stage the rooted cuttings can either be sold to a wholesale nursery or they may be planted out and grown on to maturity. Alternatively young 'liners' can be bought in and grown on to point of sale, a great deal of activity in this sphere is now taking place in the UK with, in many cases, sources of liners on the Continent. Some species will make saleable plants within one year, while others will need several years.

Production per acre

Average no cuttings planted	100,000
Less wastage—20%	20,000
Total plants produced	80,000

Approximate costs per acre

Peat-mulch—20 tons @ £6	120
Fertiliser—8cwt @ £2	16
Sprays @ £2.5/1,000	250
Labels @ £1.5/1,000 produced	120
Labour—1,450 hours @ 60p	870
Tractor—337 hours @ 35p	118
Total cost	£1,494

Labour requirement and cost per acre

Job	Rate of Work	No of units	Labour hours	Rate/ hour p	Total Cost £
Spreading peat		1 acre	8	60	5
Ploughing		1 acre	2	60	1
Spreading fertiliser		1 acre	1	60	1
Cultivation		1 acre	6	60	4
Planting cuttings	120/hour	100,000	833	60	500
Cultivation & spraying			120	60	72
Lifting (machine)	250/hour	80,000	320	60	192
Grading and packing	500/hour	80,000	160	60	95
			1,450		£870

M

Average cost of growing on per 1,000 shrubs produced = £18.70

Summary costs, returns and margins of shrubs per 1,000 plants

	Quick-growing shrubs (1) *	Slow-growing shrubs (2) *
Propagation	£	£
Value of rooted cuttings & layers	65	120
Less costs of propagation	10	20
Margin over propagating costs	55	100
Typical propagation period	1–3 months	6–10 months
Growing on		
Wholesale value of shrubs	200	400
Less Costs of propagation (as above)	10	20
Costs of growing on	19	19
Total production costs	29	39
Margin over production costs	171	361
Typical production period	1 year	3 years
Margin per year per 1,000 plants	£171	£120

Summary of typical costs per 1,000 shrubs produced for quick- and slow-rooting species using different methods of propagation

	Quick-Rooting Species			Slow-Rooting Species		
		Frames or plastic			Frames or plastic	
Method of Propagation	Outdoor	tunnels	Mist	Outdoor	tunnels	Mist
Cuttings rooted	60%	80%	90%	25%	40%	50%
Cost of propagation/1,000 shrub liners produced	£ 8.7	£11.4	£16.2	£20.8	£22.8	£29.1
Add Cost of growing liners to maturity	£18.7	£18.7	£18.7	£18.7	£18.7	£18.7
Total cost per 1,000 shrubs produced	£27.4	£30.1	£34.9	£39.5	£41.5	£47.8

* eg (1) Forsythia, deutzia, hypericum, ribes, etc.
(2) conifers, rhododendrons, etc.

Propagation from Seed

Propagation of trees and shrubs from seed is such a varied technique because of vastly different germination processes, different prices for seed (which can differ enormously) and last but not least the extremely variable germination periods and percentages, that no economic figures have been given. *In general* costs will not be vastly different to propagation from cuttings.

BUSH ROSES

The production of roses requires specialist skill in the method of grafting. This is done by cutting a T-shaped opening in the bark of the stock plant (eg rosa canina or dog rose) then inserting a bud, tying it securely in place with vinyl tape. Rosa canina seedlings are usually bought in from specialist raisers and planted out from November to March. Bud wood can also be purchased and stocks are budded the following summer. The bushes will be ready for sale during winter one year after budding.

Production per acre

No of seedlings planted	30,000
yielding Grade 1 bushes—60%	18,000
Grade 2 bushes—30%	9,000
Grade 3 bushes—10%	3,000

Period of production: 2 years.

Costs and returns per acre

		Total £	Per annum £
Revenue—18,000 @ £140/1,000	£2,520		
9,000 @ £85/1,000	765		
		3,285	1,642

Less crop expenses:

Seedlings—30,000 @ £16/1,000	£480		
Bud wood—30,000 @ £15/1,000	450		
Farmyard manure—25 tons @ £1.5	38		
Fertiliser—8cwt @ £2	16		
Sprays, tying materials—estimated	75		
Labels, etc—estimated	45		
Labour—661 hours @ 60p	397		
Tractor—317 hours @ 35p	111		
		1,612	806

Margin per acre   £1,673   £836
Cost per 1,000 bushes produced: £62

Labour requirement and cost

Date	Job	Rate of Work	No of units	Labour hours	Rate/ hour	Total Cost £
1st year						
Oct/Nov	Spread manure		1 acre	8	60p	5
,,	Plough		1 acre	2	60p	1
,,	Spread fertiliser		1 acre	1	60p	1
,,	Cultivation		1 acre	6	60p	4
,,	Plant seedlings (machine)	500/hour	30,000	60	60p	36
Mar/June	Spraying & cultivation			49	60p	29
July/Aug	Budding & tying	120/hour	30,000	250	60p	150
2nd year						
Oct/Feb	Spread fertiliser		1 acre	1	60p	1
Mar	Cutting back	750/hour	30,000	40	60p	24
Apr/July	Spraying & cultivating			70	60p	42
3rd year						
Oct/Feb	Lifting (machine)	250/hour	30,000	120	60p	72
	Grading & packing	500/hour	27,000	54	60p	32
				661		£397

STANDARD ROSES

To produce standard roses, stems of rosa rugosa are bought in and planted from November to March. The stems are budded in the same way as for bush roses during the following summer. The standards are lifted during the winter one year after budding.

Production per acre

No of stems planted	12,500
yielding Grade 1—60%	7,500
Grade 2—25%	3,200
Grade 3—15%	1,800

Costs and returns per acre

		Total £	Per annum £
Revenue—7,500 @ £750/1,000	£5,625		
3,200 @ £300/1,000	960	6,585	3,292
Less crop expenses:			
Rugosa stems—12,500 @ £300/1,000		3,750	
Bud wood—12,500 @ £15/1,000		188	
Farmyard manure—25 tons @ £1.5		38	
Fertiliser—8cwt @ £2		16	
Sprays, tying material—estimated		31	
Labels, etc—estimated		19	
Stakes—5,000 @ 15p		750	
Labour—1,035 hours @ 60p		621	
Tractor—200 hours @ 35p		70	
		5,483	2,744
Margin per acre		£1,102	£548

Labour requirement and cost

Date	Job	Rate of Work	No of units	Labour hours	Rate/ hour p	Total Cost £
1st year						
Oct/Mar	Spreading manure and cultivating			17	60	15
,,	Planting rugosa stems	38/hour	12,500	329	60	198
,,	Staking	25/hour	5,000	200	60	120
Mar/May	Spraying and cultivating			52	60	31
June	Budding and tying	120/hour	12,500	104	60	63
2nd year						
Oct/Mar	Heading off	250/hour	12,500	50	60	30
Mar/July	Cultivating and side shooting			133	60	80
3rd year						
Oct/Feb	Lifting (machine)	125/hour	12,500	100	60	60
	Grading & packing	250/hour	12,500	50	60	30
				1,035		£627

CONTAINERISATION

Containerisation is a vital part of tree, shrub and rose production in order to allow extended sale throughout the year. Costs for containerisation are roughly as follows per 1,000 shrubs (of medium size):

Cost of containers @ £6/1,000	£6
Labour—33 hours @ 60p	£20
	£26

To this must be added the cost of the compost.

MISCELLANEOUS ITEMS

Turf

There can be an excellent demand for turf of which there are three basic forms:

1. *Seawashed turf*: usually of fine-stem indigenous fescues and bent grasses; it can be of high quality and remarkably free from weeds.

2. *Moorland turf*: produced on high elevated areas, the grass is of poorer quality and there can be weed problems.

3. *Field turf*: tends to be of much lower quality and can contain a wide range of grasses and weeds.

All turf can be treated with hormone weedkiller and fertiliser and is lifted by hired turf-lifting machine and sold on a per sq yd basis.

Herbaceous and Rock Plants
There is scope for the production of herbaceous and rock plants, which can be propagated both from seed and from cuttings (also by division). In broad terms, the economic picture is as described for young shrub production (pages 179–184).

MARKETING OF NURSERY STOCK (hardy or otherwise)
Retail selling of trees and shrubs tends to be in the hands of garden centres and while it is certainly possible to link production to garden-centre operation, one then becomes involved in fairly large capital investment. It may of course be possible to supply existing garden centres with trees and shrubs at wholesale prices, or alternatively join a group of producers and feed supplies to them on schedule and to certain specifications, so that the producers' group can offer a wide range of items to garden centres. The same is true of supplying New Town complexes or local authorities.

Alternatively one can stay independent and build up a wholesale supply business for a certain range of items, and the same is true of retail trade, a combination of both being the compromise which many small producers aim at. When one has a landscape business or is associated with one, this will also serve as an excellent outlet for nursery stock.

With the rapid escalation of shrub and tree production, particularly in easily produced lines such as ericas, we cannot stress too strongly the need for securing market outlets before becoming too deeply involved in nursery stock production. Nor can the need for *consistent quality* be overstressed, as we can see little demand for rubbish.

Summary of Yields, Margins and Packaging Requirements

Key

M(a) Margins per acre
M(f) Margins per 1,000sq ft
M(h) Margins per hour
P   Packaging (for wholesale markets unless indicated otherwise)
TY   Target yields per 1,000sq ft
TY(a) Target yields per acre

OUTDOOR VEGETABLE CROPS

Asparagus: TY(a) 30cwt; M(a) £514; M(h) £1.10; P lettuce crates, 20 bundles per crate

Beans (French): TY(a) 2½ tons; M(a) £146; M(h) £0.54; P cardboard boxes, 8lb per box

Beans (runner): TY(a) 5 tons; M(a) £340; M(h) £0.55; P cardboard boxes, 8lb per box

Beetroot: TY(a) 14 tons; M(a) £164; M(h) £0.59; P 28lb nets

Brussels sprouts: TY(a) 4 tons; M(a) £108; M(h) £0.51; P nets, 20lb per net

Carrots: TY(a) 15 tons; M(a) £123; M(h) £0.61; P 28lb nets

Cauliflower (early): TY(a) 9,000 head; M(a) £219; M(h) £0.58; P lettuce crates, 6–8 per crate.

(summer and autumn): TY(a) 7,000 head; M(a) £98; M(h) £0.50; P lettuce crates, 6–8 per crate (winter): TY(a) 5,000 head; M(a) £109; M(h) £0.63; P lettuce crates, 6–8 per crate

Celery (self-blanching): TY(a) 8,500 bundles; M(a) £379; M(h) £0.32; P cardboard boxes, 4 bundles per box

(main crop): TY(a) 8,500 bundles; M(a) £302; M(h) £0.40; P cardboard boxes, 4 bundles per box

Leeks: TY(a) 10 tons; M(a) £357; M(h) £0.73; P lettuce crates, 18lb per crate

Lettuce (early transplanted): TY(a) 36,000 head; M(a) £693; M(h) £1.23; P lettuce crates, 20 per crate

(summer): TY(a) 20,000 head; M(a) £180; M(h) £0.82; P lettuce crates, 18–24 per crate

Onions: TY(a) 14 tons; M(a) £408; M(h) £2.08; P nets, 56lb

Salad onions (syboes): TY(a) 5 tons; M(a) £368; M(h) £0.37; P cardboard boxes, 8lb per box

Parsley: TY(a) 15,000lb; M(a) £558; M(h) £2.92; P cardboard boxes, 4lb per box

Radish: TY(a) 3,500doz bunches; M(a) £830; M(h) £2.40; P 12 × 1doz bunches per box

Rhubarb: TY(a) 12 tons; M(a) £271; M(h) £1.00; P lettuce crates, 1½ stone per crate

Turnip (early): TY(a) 400doz bunches; M(a) £250; M(h) £0.96; P lettuce crates, 4 bunches per crate

VEGETABLE CROPS UNDER GLASS

Tomatoes: TY 24cwt, ie 220 boxes × 12lb; M(f) £97; M(h) £0.74; P cardboard boxes, 12lb per box lined with paper

Lettuce (winter): TY 1,600 head; M(f) £27; M(h) £0.80; P cardboard boxes, 12 per box in polythene bags

(early spring): TY 1,800 head; M(f) £25; M(h) £0.83; P cardboard boxes, 12 per box in polythene bags (late spring): TY 1,900 head; M(f) £42; M(h) £1.62; P lettuce crates, 18–24 per crate

Total: TY 5,300 head; M(f) £94; M(h) £1.04

Cucumber: TY 5,000; M(f) £139; M(h) £0.40; P cardboard boxes, 14 per box

Rhubarb (forced): TY 2 tons per 1,000sq ft of glass or forcing shed; M(f) £168; M(h) £1.19; P lettuce crates, $1\frac{1}{2}$ stone per crate

Peppers: TY 120 boxes × 12lb; M(f) £115; M(h) £0.73

Mushrooms: TY 3lb per sq ft of bed area; M(f) £910; M(h) £0.73; P cardboard baskets, 3lb per basket

Strawberries (under glass): TY 2 tons per acre; M(a) £1,328; M(h) £1.36; P $\frac{1}{4}$lb punnets and trays

FRUIT CROPS

Apples (cooking): TY(a) 300 bushels; M(a) £167; M(h) £0.70; P bushel boxes, 40lb

Apples (dessert): TY(a) 300 bushels; M(a) £368; M(h) £1.20; P half-bushel boxes, 20lb

Blackcurrants: TY(a) 2 tons; M(a) £225; M(h) £0.70; P supplied by processors

Gooseberries: TY(a) $3\frac{1}{2}$ tons; M(a) £260; M(h) £0.70; P cardboard boxes, 12lb per box

Plums: TY(a) 9,600lb; M(a) £322; M(h) £1.80; P cardboard boxes, 12lb per box

Raspberries: TY(a) 2 tons; M(a) £362; M(h) £0.36; P chips, 2lb per chip

Strawberries: TY(a) 2 tons 5cwt; M(a) £585; M(h) £0.59; P chips, 2lb per chip

CUT FLOWERS OUTDOORS

Asters: TY(a) 30,000 bunches × 12; M(a) £825; M(h) £0.55; P cardboard boxes, 24 bunches per box

Anemones: TY(a) 20,000 bunches; M(a) £629; M(h) £0.52;
  P cardboard boxes, 15 bunches per box
Chrysanthemums: TY(a) 8,500 bunches × 6; M(a) £1,559;
  M(h) £0.79; P cardboard boxes, 5 bunches per box
Daffodils: TY(a) 1,260 bunches × 10; M(a) £357; M(h) £0.76;
  P cardboard boxes, 24 bunches per box
Dahlias: TY(a) 20,000 bunches × 6; M(a) £653; M(h) £0.34;
  P cardboard boxes, 20 bunches per box
Pyrethrums: TY(a) 1,200 bunches × 12; M(a) £498; M(h)
  £1.07; P cardboard boxes, 36 bunches per box
Stocks: TY(a) 7,000 bunches × 6; M(a) £1,151; M(h) £1.53;
  P cardboard boxes, 8 bunches per box
Sweet William: TY(a) 30,000 bunches; M(a) £1,085; M(h)
  £0.61; P cardboard boxes, 18 bunches per box
Tulips: TY(a) 2,700 bunches × 6; M(a) £537; M(h) £0.80;
  P cardboard boxes, 16 bunches per box

ORNAMENTAL GLASSHOUSE CROPS

Bedding plants: TY 2,000 boxes; M(f) £783; M(h) £0.95;
  P in boxes to shops or retail

Bulbs
Daffodils (forced): TY 3 tons—12,000 bunches; M(f) £337;
  M(h) £0.48; P flower-boxes, 20 bunches per box
Tulips (forced): TY 90% cut—10,800 bunches; M(f) £391;
  M(h) £0.55; P flower-boxes, 20 bunches per box
Tulips (direct-planted): TY 92% cut—2,220 bunches; M(f)
  £129; M(h) £1.37; P flower-boxes, 20 bunches per box
Hyacinths (Christmas): TY 1,900 bowls; M(f) £180; M(h)
  £1.16; P cardboard boxes, 6 per box

Chrysanthemums (direct-planted)
Single-stem: TY 4,000 blooms; M(f) £78; M(h) £1.30; P
  chrysanthemum boxes, 4–6 bunches per box

Two-stem: TY 3,000 blooms; M(f) £78; M(h) £1.16; P chrysanthemum boxes, 4–6 bunches per box

Three-stem: TY 3,000 blooms; M(f) £71; M(h) £1.00; P chrysanthemum boxes, 4–6 bunches per box

Sprays: TY 4,000 blooms; M(f) £78; M(h) £1.10; P chrysanthemum boxes, 24 sprays per box

Lifted crop: TY 3,900 blooms; M(f) £153; M(h) £0.67; P chrysanthemum boxes, 5 bunches of 6

Pot Plants

Chrysanthemums (Christmas): TY 712 pots; M(f) £18; M(h) £0.10; P cellophane sleeves, 6 pots per box

Chrysanthemums (all-year): TY 3,078 pots; M(f) £141; M(h) £0.22; P cellophane sleeves, 6 pots per box

Poinsettias: TY 1,620 pots; M(f) £179; M(h) £0.83; P cardboard boxes, 8 per box

Azalea indica (small): TY 1,800 pots; M(f) £174; M(h) £0.61; P cardboard boxes, 8 per box

Azalea indica (medium): TY 720 pots; M(f) £309; M(h) £2.71; P cardboard boxes, 6 per box

Azalea indica (large): TY 450 pots; M(f) £125; M(h) £1.74; P cardboard boxes, 5 per box

Cyclamen: TY 720 pots; M(f) £175; M(h) £0.88; P cardboard boxes, 6 per box

Perlargoniums & geraniums: TY 1,980 pots; M(f) £226; M(h) £1.90; P cardboard boxes, 12 per box, cellophane sleeve

Cinerareas: TY 720 pots; M(f) £91; M(h) £0.74; P cardboard boxes, 8 per box

Foliage plants: TY 2,700 plants; M(h) £109; M(f) £0.73; P cardboard boxes, 18 per box

Carnations: TY 20,000 stems over 18–21 months; M(f) £85

Freesias: TY 4,000 bunches; M(f) £181; M(h) £0.63; P cardboard boxes, 24 bunches per box

Roses: TY 887 bunches × 12 (average over 10 years); M(f) £201

Summary of Labour Requirements (Hours)

KEY: J January, F February, Mh March, A April, M May, J June, Jy July, Au August, S September, O October, N November, D December.

OUTDOOR VEGETABLE CROPS

Crop	Total	J	F	Mh	A	M	J	Jy	Au	S	O	N	D
Asparagus:	477	—	29	1	17	182	182	1	2	—	25	19	19
Beans (French):	270	—	—	3	12	40	25	180	10	—	—	—	—
(runner):	615	—	—	—	110	40	30	65	140	100	20	80	30
Beetroot:	303	—	3	8	6	4	72	150	60	—	—	—	—
Brussels sprouts:	227	30	21	18	—	20	14	2	5	—	18	36	63
Carrots:	202	8	9	9	8	9	4	7	15	18	38	39	38
Cauliflower (early):	380	40	20	85	60	25	50	15	—	—	45	20	20
(summer and autumn):	195	—	—	—	17	31	28	69	40	10	—	—	—
(winter):	169	—	—	10	50	50	30	5	20	—	—	4	—
Celery (self-blanching):	1,190	30	110	20	320	200	45	25	750	220	—	20	50
(main crop):	748	22	60	75	50	50	65	55	19	17	55	110	170
(frames or plastic tunnels):	748	62	62	75	50	50	65	55	19	17	55	110	170
Leeks:	519	62	62	34	1	108	105	3	6	16	30	30	62
Lettuce (early transplanted):	554	101	91	2	62	90	98	46	46	—	—	—	—
(summer):	218	—	2	2	12	66	48	10	8	10	—	—	—
Onions:	198	—	2	2	—	4	2	10	8	10	—	—	160
Salad Onions (syboes):	987	—	8	6	9	167	323	480	—	—	—	—	—
Parsley:	191	9	10	19	18	14	26	25	28	15	12	8	9
Radish:	345	—	25	10	110	120	80	—	—	—	—	—	—
Rhubarb:	272	35	31	31	30	42	35	22	—	—	2	40	37
Turnip (early):	260	—	3	10	15	90	120	22	—	—	—	—	—

197

VEGETABLES UNDER GLASS (per 1,000sq ft)

Crop	Total	J	F	Mh	A	M	J	Jy	Au	S	O	N	D
Tomatoes:	131	4	8	15	17	10	24	18	16	10	2	5	2
Lettuce (winter):	34	—	—	—	—	—	—	—	5	14	1	1	13
(early spring):	30	14	2	14	—	—	—	—	—	—	—	—	—
(late spring):	26	—	—	5	11	10	—	—	—	—	—	—	—
Total:	90	14	2	19	11	10	—	—	5	14	1	1	13
Cucumber:	342	12	15	25	45	45	40	40	40	35	20	15	10
Rhubarb (forced):	141	64	28	1	6	—	—	—	—	—	—	9	28
Peppers:													
Mushrooms:	1,250					25 hours per week							
Strawberries (per acre)													
(under glass):	977	10	110	120	450	190	36	—	—	36	—	12	13

FRUIT CROPS (per acre)

Crop	Total	J	F	Mh	A	M	J	Jy	Au	S	O	N	D
Apples (cooking):	240	15	15	5	5	8	4	6	2	40	20	10	110
(dessert):	315	30	30	10	10	10	15	10	5	45	50	5	95
Blackcurrants:	320	20	—	10	4	8	20	80	115	3	—	40	20
Gooseberries:	375	30	15	15	60	—	10	80	85	5	5	20	50
Plums:	180	—	5	10	5	5	5	35	55	50	10	—	—
Raspberries:	992	10	10	60	12	5	15	420	400	30	10	10	10
Strawberries:	986	11	11	21	111	90	198	457	36	12	13	13	13

CUT FLOWERS OUTDOORS (per acre)

Crop	Total	J	F	Mh	A	M	J	Jy	Au	S	O	N	D
Asters:	1,518	100	90	20	80	10	8	600	600	—	—	—	—
Anemones:	1,217	—	20	15	22	25	40	35	100	270	360	250	80
Chrysanthemums:	1,970	150	110	70	50	300	170	120	100	350	350	200	—
Daffodils:	466	—	—	—	—	—	—	—	—	—	—	—	—
Dahlias:	1,910	10	100	40	30	150	200	300	300	300	335	135	10
Pyrethrums:	465	—	50	25	35	50	250	25	—	—	15	15	—
Stocks:	754	—	2	2	155	125	60	170	150	80	5	5	—
Sweet William:	1,775	—	7	17	17	702	802	30	50	150	—	—	—
Tulips:	673	—	—	—	—	—	—	—	—	—	—	—	—

ORNAMENTAL GLASSHOUSE CROPS

Crop	Total	J	F	Mh	A	M	J	Jy	Au	S	O	N	D
Bedding plants:	828	12	147	246	272	127	24	—	—	—	—	—	—
Bulbs													
Daffodils (forced):	705	15	75	90	150	—	—	—	—	—	210	15	150
Tulips (forced):	660	15	72	88	145	—	—	—	—	—	180	15	145
(direct planted):	95	—	—	—	—	—	—	—	—	—	5	10	80
Hyacinths (Christmas):	155	—	—	—	—	—	—	—	—	30	20	5	100
Direct-planted chrysanthemums (single-stem):	60	—	—	—	—	—	—	—	15	5	15	5	20
2-stem:	70	—	—	—	—	—	—	15	10	5	15	5	20
3-stem:	70	—	—	—	—	—	—	15	10	5	15	5	20
Sprays:	70	—	—	—	—	—	—	15	10	5	15	5	20
Lifted crop:	227	15	11	7	5	30	17	12	10	37	24	36	23
Pot plants													
Chrysanthemums (Christmas):	175	—	—	—	—	—	—	—	—	50	40	40	45
(all-year):	650	13 hours per week											
Poinsettias:	216	—	—	—	—	—	—	40	25	13	13	13	112
Azalea indica (small):	286	—	—	—	—	—	2	10	12	62	60	52	88
(medium):	114	—	—	—	—	—	1	4	5	25	24	20	35
(large):	72	—	—	—	—	—	1	2	3	16	15	13	22
Cyclamen:	198	6	2	25	2	3	26	18	21	19	18	17	41
Pelargoniums & geraniums:	119	8	8	18	19	3	—	—	9	15	34	2	3
Cinerarias:	123	—	—	—	—	—	—	6	6	31	23	19	38
Foliage plants:	150	3 hours per week											
Freesias:	288	—	—	40	30	5	5	5	5	37	10	79	72

Appendices

1 GROWING-ROOM ECONOMICS

Utilisation factors, capital and running costs, based
on Electricity Council Handbook No 1—Growing Rooms

The desirability of crops being grown under 'standard' conditions of light and temperature have been referred to earlier, and the chief reason why cheaper forms of 'growing rooms' have been developed has been to lower capital costs. A six-bench 'standard' growing room with approximately 168sq ft of growing area will cost £850 (excluding benches), which taken over an average of eight years is an annual cost of £106. Interest on half the capital cost would add another £34, making a final cost of £140 pa. If $\frac{2}{3}$ of the growing area is used throughout the year, the cost per sq ft per day will therefore be .0035p, and this cost would rise for less frequent usage.

Running costs, including electric power and fluorescent tube replacement work out at about .28p per sq ft, and the cost of raising various plants can be calculated as follows. It is repeated that considerable developments are taking place all the time regarding growing rooms and supplementary and reflected light, and growers are strongly advised to keep up to date through the trade papers and journals.

Costs per sq ft/day
Running cost	0.28p
Fixed cost (assuming 50% space utilisation)	0.005p
	0.285p

	Cost of Treatment
Tomatoes—16 plants/sq ft—21 days	.388p per plant
Lettuce—1 box seedlings/sq ft—3 days	.855p/box or
	.018p/plant
Bedding plants—1 box/sq ft—ave 6 days	1.71p/box
French marigolds—2 days	.57p/box
Lobelia—10 days	2.85p/box

2   CAPITAL COSTS OF EQUIPMENT

Owing to the rapid price fluctuations and wide range of equipment, these prices are merely given for guidance; they cannot be precisely accurate.

Machinery

Cultivating Equipment

Ploughs, 2 furrow, £120–150; 3 furrow, £175–225; 4 furrow, £230–320.

Cultivators, 7–11ft, £120–220; 8–15ft spring type, £100–200.

Harrows, 7–20ft, £35–90.

Disc harrows, 6–8ft, £140–180.

Rollers, 8ft, £110–150.

Fertiliser distributors, disc type, 8–12ft, £160–200; spinner, £55–150; hand-spinner, £17.

Sprayers, hand-knapsack, £3–20; hand-propelled, engine-driven, £60–185; tractor-driven, low volume, £85–120; tractor-driven, high/low volume, £160–460.

Transplanter, 2–3 row, £200–300.

Spaced seed driller, single seed units, £30 upwards; 4–6 row, £200–275.

Garden Tractors and Rotovators

2-wheeled rotovator, small, £90–160; large, £260–300.

4-wheeled tractors, light market-garden type, £1,200–1,500.

Other Equipment and Tools

Tractor fork-lift, £400.

Barrows, hand, £5–10.

Trolleys, hand, £25–35; powered, £200–300.

Soil shredders, £100–300.

Soil block machines, hand-operated, £20; automatic 2,800 blocks/hour, £250.

Soil sterilisers, powered, £200–300; hand-operated, $\frac{1}{2}$cu ft, £11; hand-operated, 1–2 bushels, £30–54.

Chain saws, 12–16in bar and chain, £78–90.

Tomato graders, automatic, £225.

Hedge cutters, complete, £15–90.

Hand tools, spades, forks, hoes, etc, £1.50–£2 each.

Glasshouses, Plastic Structures and Equipment

Glasshouses

Small garden types, timber/alloy 50–100sq ft (price does not include erection) £55–110.

Venlo, timber cladding, metal framework (price includes ventilation and erection) £320 per 1,000sq ft.

Wide-span houses, aluminium—22ft span upwards (price includes ventilation and erection) £480 per 1,000sq ft.

Mobile houses, add approx 20% to above prices.

Frames

Dutch-light type, 5 × 2ft per light, simply constructed using sleepers and sides, £120 per 1,000sq ft.

Plastic Structures

Polythene cloches, including polythene cladding, 1$\frac{1}{2}$–3p/sq ft.

Plastic tunnels, 14–20ft span including polythene cladding, 4–10p/sq ft.

Polythene tunnels with fan ventilation, 20ft span upwards, including polythene cladding, 15–20p/sq ft.

Polythene cladding (replacement required every two years), £5.30/1,000sq ft.

Benches, aluminium, 60p per sq ft; timber with metal supports, 45p per sq ft.

Heating

Boilers, 175,000–1,250,000btu/hour, 35sec oil, £224–760; ditto, natural gas, £420–988; second-hand, 60,000–250,000btu/hour, oil-fired, £120-250.

Piping, 1¼in, £2,500 per acre; 3in mains, £250 per acre.

Solid fuel boiler and pipes for small houses, £30–40 (very variable).

Oil tanks, 500–3,000gal capacity, £50–200.

Space Heaters

Paraffin hot-air burners, for houses up to 18 × 9ft, £3–16.

Tubular heaters, 2–12ft, 120–720 watts for small houses, £3–8.

Electric water heater, for houses up to 12 × 8ft, £23.

Fan heaters, 1,250–3,000 watts, thermostatic control, for small houses, £12–17.

Oil-fired warm-air heaters, 30–60,000btu/hour with ducting, £80–130; 100–150,000btu/hour with ducting, £150–200; 300–500,000btu/hour with ducting, £450–660.

Soil Warming

Warming cables, 20–534ft, 75–2,000 watts, £4–22.

Soil thermostat, 15 amps, £6.

Soil thermometer, for sterilising and propagating, £1.

Control Equipment

Thermostat, £7.15.

Aspirated screen, 2–4 thermostats, £25–31.

Fuels: *Comparative Cost and Efficiency*

Fuel	Calorific Value	Efficiency	Price of fuel	Cost per useful therm*
Coal	12–14,000btu/lb	65%	£12–14/ton	70p
Oil 35sec	20,000btu/gal	80%	8p	50p
„ 200sec	19,000btu/gal	80%	7p	46p
„ 950sec	18,500btu/gal	80%	6p	41p

Prices of oil do not take into account the rebate of 1p per gallon claimable by commercial growers.

Ventilation

Automatic expansion ventilation gear for wooden houses, £6.35; ditto for metal houses, £8.20–8.90.

Fan ventilation, 9–48in thermostatic control, £22–120.

Irrigation

Trickle irrigation, complete, £1,125/acre.

Spraylines, complete, £1,000–1,400/acre.

Volmatic, for tomatoes, 7p per plant; for cucumbers, 12p per plant; for capillary benches, 36p per sq m bench area; pots on benches, 5–8p per pot, depending on spacing.

Storage tanks, 5,000–7,500gal capacity, £120–150.

Pumps, £100–150.

Diluters, low-pressure, ½–5gal, £5–8; up to 1,000gal/hour, 2–6gal, £15–24; up to 3,000gal/hour, 9–36gal, £35–70.

Propagation Equipment

Mist units, single-nozzle, £45; extension nozzle plus pipework, £4.50 per nozzle.

*Therm = 100,000btu.

Capital costs per 1,000sq ft

	Total Cost	Est. life	Annual cost
Mist nozzles and pipework—			
76 @ £3	£228	5 years	£46
Control unit	45	8 years	6
*Soil-warming cables—1,600ft @ 30p	48	5 years	10
Control unit	25	8 years	3
Benches—800sq ft @ 20p	160	10 years	16
Trays—for 2 batches, 1,600 @ 5p	80	4 years	20
Glasshouse and heating equipment	700	10 years	70
	£1,286		£171

Propagators, Humex Ltd, 4ft 2in × 2ft 2in, with bottom heat and air warming £66.40; ditto with bottom heat only, £43.20; ditto with glass or plastic dome, £29.20–32.20; control unit, £16–20; small propagator with plastic cover, £5.20.

Irradiation lamps, 400 watts, £20–25.

Contract Hire Charges, per day

Rotovator—2-wheel tractors, £3–7; tractor mounted, 6ft, £10.

Soil shredder, £3.50.

Chain saws, 1-man portable, £2.50.

Tree pruner, 10ft long, £0.50.

Land leveller, £3.50.

Fertiliser distributor, push type, £0.50.

Sprayers, 50gal, 8ft spray boom, £4; 4gal knapsack, £0.75.

Garden rollers, £0.75.

Soil-Sterilisation Costs

Own steriliser, 1gal per ton, 8p per ton.

Hire of steam boiler for glasshouses, £4 per 1,000sq ft; 60gal oil @ 8p, £4.80 per 1,000sq ft.

Methyl bromide, contract charge, £15 per 1,000sq ft.

Metham sodium, 8lb per 1,000sq ft, £3 per 1,000sq ft.

*Or mini-bore systems (cost indefinite).

3 TRAINING COURSES

Degree Courses in Horticulture (abbreviations key at end of list)

	Course offered	Duration (years)	Remarks
Bath University of Technology, Bath.	BSc Hons	4 SW	Honours degree
University of London,	BSc	3	
Wye College, Ashford, Kent.	MPhil	2	By research
	PhD	3	By research
University of Nottingham.	BSc	3	Ordinary or Honours
School of Agriculture, Sutton	MPhil	1 or 2	By research
Bonnington, Loughborough,	PhD	2 (min)	By research
Leicestershire.			
University of Reading,	BSc	3	
Faculty of Agriculture,	BSc Hons	3	
London Road, Reading.	MSc	1	
	MPhil	2	Food science
	PhD	3	Food science
University of Strathclyde, Royal College Building, Glasgow, in association with the West of Scotland Agricultural College, Auchincruive, Ayr.	BSc Hons	4	

Higher National Diploma Courses

Essex Institute of Agriculture, Writtle, Nr. Chelmsford.	HND	3 SW	

Approved Courses at Further Education Establishments

Isle of Ely College of	NC	1 FT	General horticulture
Further Education and	X	1 FT	Floristry and flower growing
Horticulture, Remnoth Road, Wisbech, Cambs.	X	1 FT	Horticulture course for those aged 15+
Cheshire College of Agriculture, Raseheath, Nantwich.	X	1 SW	Parks and recreation provision
Essex Institute of Agriculture, Writtle, Nr. Chelmsford.	ND	1 FT	Final National Diploma in Horticulture (RHS)
	OND	3 SW	Amenity horticulture
	OND	3 SW	Commercial horticulture
Hertfordshire College of	NC	1 FT	
Agriculture & Horticulture,	S	1 FT	Glasshouse production
Oaklands, St. Albans.	S	12wks	Horticultural management

	Course offered	Duration (years)	Remarks
	OND	3 SW	Commercial horticulture
	OND	3 SW	Glasshouse production
Hadlow College of Agriculture and Horticulture, Hadlow, Tonbridge.	NC	1 FT	
	S	1 FT	Fruit growing
	S	1 FT	Plant nursery practice and management
	S	1 FT	Crop production under glass
	OND	3 SW	Commercial horticulture
Lancashire College of Agriculture, Hutton, Preston.	NC	1 FT	Amenity horticulture
	OND	3 SW	Amenity horticulture
Waterperry School of Horticulture, Wheatley, Oxford.	ND	2 FT	Leads (after experience) to NDH (Part 1)
Somerset College of Agriculture, Hutton, Preston. Cannington, Nr. Bridgwater.	NC	1 FT	Commercial horticulture
	NC	1 FT	Amenity horticulture
	S	1 FT	Amenity horticulture (advanced NCH)
Merrist Wood Agricultural College, Worplesdon, Nr. Guildford.	NC	1 FT	Nursery and ornamental horticulture
	X	1 FT	Landscape construction
	X	1 FT	
	X	10wks	Tree surgery and arboriculture
	OND	3 SW	Commercial horticulture (options in Arboriculture, Landscape, Nursery practice)
Pershore College of Horticulture, Avonbank, Pershore.	NC	1 FT	
	S	1 FT	Leads (after experience) to NDH
	S	1 FT	Market gardening
	OND	3 SW	Plant nursery practice
	OND	3 SW	Commercial horticulture
The Askham Bryan College of Agriculture & Horticulture, Askham Bryan, York.	NC	1 FT	
	S	1 FT	Recreational and decorative horticulture
	OND	3 SW	Amenity horticulture
Flintshire College of Horticulture, Northop.	NC	1 FT	
	S	1 FT	Horticultural enterprises in farm rotation
	X	1 FT	Floristry with flower production

	Course offered	Duration (years)	Remarks
	X	1 FT	Course for juniors of 15+
	X	2 SW	Floristry with flower production
	X	1 SW	Commercial vegetable production
The Monmouthshire College of Agriculture, Usk.	X		Course for juniors of 15+—non-residential
The West of Scotland Agricultural College, Auchincruive, Ayr.	OND	3 SW	Amenity horticulture
	OND	3 SW	Commercial and general horticulture

Training is also available at Edinburgh and Kew Botanic Gardens, involving 3 year courses.

KEY
OND = Ordinary National Diploma
ND = National Diploma
NC = National Certificate
S   = Supplementary
X   = Courses not leading to the above qualifications
FT = Full Time
SW = Sandwich

With acknowledgements to *The Commercial Grower*

4 TRADE PAPERS

Commercial Grower, Sovereign Way, Tonbridge, Kent.
The Grower, 49 Doughty Street, London.
Gardeners Chronicle & Horticultural Trade Journal, Gillow House, 5 Winsley Street, London.
Nurseryman & Garden Centre, Sovereign Way, Tonbridge, Kent.

5 CONVERSION TABLES

(a) Metric Conversion Factors

1 acre	= 0·40 hectares		1 hectare	= 2·47 acres
1 yard	= 0·91 metres		1 metre	= 1·09 yards
1 ton	= 1·02 tonnes		1 tonne	= 0·98 tons
1 cwt	= 50·8 kilogrammes		1 kilogramme	= 0·020cwt
1 lb	= 0·45 kilogrammes		1 kilogramme	= 2·20lb
1 gallon	= 4·55 litres		1 litre	= 0·22 gallons
1 pint	= 0·57 litres		1 litre	= 1·76 pints

(b) Rates of application, yields, etc

Rate per acre cwt	Rate per sq yd oz	Rate per hectare Kg
1	0·4	125
2	0·8	251
3	1·2	376
4	1·6	502
5	2·0	627
10	4·0	1,255
15	6·0	1,882
20	8·0	2,511
30	12·0	3,766
40	16·0	5,022
50	20·0	6,277

(c) Temperature—Fahrenheit/Celsius scale

Fahrenheit °F	Celsius °C	Celsius °C	Fahrenheit °F
20	− 6·7	0	32
30	− 1·1	10	50
40	4·4	15	59
50	10·0	20	68
60	15·6	25	77
70	21·1	30	86
80	26·7		

(d) Land Measure

1 acre = 4,840 square yards = 43,560 square feet
1 square yard = 9 square feet = 144 square inches

(e) Volume

1 cubic foot = 1,728 cubic inches
1 cubic yard = 27 cubic feet = 21 bushels (approximately)
1 bushel = 1·28 cubic feet

(f) Plants required per acre

Spacing	Plants per acre	Spacing	Plants per acre
6 × 6in	174,000	18 × 9in	39,000
6 × 10 ,,	105,000	18 × 12 ,,	29,000
8 × 8 ,,	98,000	18 × 18 ,,	19,000
8 × 10 ,,	78,000	24 × 12 ,,	22,000
10 × 10 ,,	63,000	24 × 18 ,,	14,500
11 × 6 ,,	95,000	24 × 24 ,,	10,900
11 × 8 ,,	91,000	30 × 12 ,,	17,400
11 × 10 ,,	57,000	30 × 18 ,,	11,600
11 × 11 ,,	52,000	30 × 24 ,,	8,700
12 × 6 ,,	87,000	30 × 30 ,,	7,000
12 × 8 ,,	65,000	36 × 18 ,,	9,700
12 × 10 ,,	52,000	36 × 24 ,,	7,300
12 × 12 ,,	44,000	36 × 30 ,,	5,800
18 × 6 ,,	58,000	36 × 36 ,,	4,800

Glossary of Terms

The use of semi-technical terms in horticultural economics cannot always be avoided. A definition of these terms is given below.

Yield: Is the quantity of marketable produce expressed per acre or per 1,000 square feet of glasshouse space. For management purposes target yields have been set based on those being achieved under suitable conditions of soil and climate and given a *reasonable* standard of crop management.

Revenue: Unless otherwise stated, *revenue is based on sales at wholesale prices.* It is the product of the wholesale price and the target yield. Obviously where retail selling is involved higher revenue can be forthcoming, but retailing costs must be taken into account.

Commission: This is the charge made by salesmen for produce sold in the wholesale markets. The charge may include handling charges in addition to the commission fee, but in either case the total charge usually amounts to about 10 per cent of total revenue.

Crop expenses: These are the costs directly attributable to a particular crop. Labour costs *have in most cases been excluded,* however, since it is assumed that most of the work will be carried out by the grower himself or by his family. Where hired labour is employed an estimate of the direct labour cost can be obtained by multiplying the total labour hours by the current wage rate. At the moment 60–70p per hour for men and 40–50p per hour for women is usual.

Margin: This is the amount left when crop expenses are deducted from revenue. It is the amount available to cover profit after charging vehicle and machinery expenses, property repairs and general expenses of running the business. *It does not include labour.*

Acknowledgements

We are grateful to our employers, The West of Scotland Agricultural College, for permission to produce this book which draws very considerably on professional experience gained over many years. We are also grateful for many sources of economic information and opinions.

For providing photographs, thanks are due to the *Scottish Field* for the plates on pages 49 (top), 67 (bottom), 68 (bottom), 136 (bottom); to Duncan McArthur for those on pages 50, 67 (top), 68 (top), 117 (bottom), 135; to the South Scotland Electricity Board, pages 117 (top), 136 (top) (photos: A. G. Ingram); to Humex Ltd, page 118 (photos: Harold King), and to Mobile Press Photos, page 49 (bottom).

Index

214